The West African Methodist Collegiate School, 1911–2021

The West African Methodist Collegiate School, 1911–2021

A Byproduct of Missionary Work in West Africa

Christopher E. S. Warburton

WIPF & STOCK · Eugene, Oregon

THE WEST AFRICAN METHODIST COLLEGIATE SCHOOL, 1911–2021
A Byproduct of Missionary Work in West Africa

Copyright © 2021 Christopher E. S. Warburton. All rights reserved. Except for brief quotations in critical publications or reviews, no part of this book may be reproduced in any manner without prior written permission from the publisher. Write: Permissions, Wipf and Stock Publishers, 199 W. 8th Ave., Suite 3, Eugene, OR 97401.

Wipf & Stock
An Imprint of Wipf and Stock Publishers
199 W. 8th Ave., Suite 3
Eugene, OR 97401

www.wipfandstock.com

PAPERBACK ISBN: 978-1-6667-0436-5
HARDCOVER ISBN: 978-1-6667-0437-2
EBOOK ISBN: 978-1-6667-0438-9

12/15/21

To the memory of my grandparents, Mr. and Mrs. J. R. Thorpe; my parents, especially my mom, Mrs. Miriam S. Warburton; my great grand uncle, the Rev. I. S. T. Fewry; Principal J. A. Garber; and my family, Conrad, Denise, and Nabia Warburton.

I have now given the preface to the history of an institution, which by God's grace should outlive several generations of its sons. It is left for others to write the chapters one by one.

—J. A. GARBER (PRINCIPAL, 1948–65)

Contents

List of Illustrations and Tables | ix
Acknowledgements | xi
Introduction | xiii

1. Historical Background of the WAM Collegiate School | 1

2. The Formative Years of the Collegiate School (1911–27) | 10
    2.1 The United Methodist Free Churches | 10
    2.2 The School and the First Principals (1911–27) | 13
    2.3 The Administration | 16
    2.4 The Boarding Department (1911–27) | 28
    2.5 The Interregnum and Mr. J. A. Garber
         (December 1927–February 1948) | 30
    2.6 The Principal, J. A. Garber, MA, LCP | 34

3. The Collegiate School at Circular Road | 36
    3.1 The School's Motto, Crest, and Song | 37
    3.2 Principal Garber and the Phase of Dire Struggle: February
         1948 to the Second Half of the 1950s | 40
    3.3 The Era of Reconstruction and the School at Wilkinson Road | 46

4. The Administration of Mr. Hastings-Spaine (1966–71) | 58
    4.1 The Administration | 58
    4.2 The Diamond Jubilee Celebrations | 65
    4.3 The Final Days of the Hastings-Spaine Administration | 71

5. The Administration of Principal Rogers-Wright (1971–78) | 72
    5.1 The Administration of Mr. Rogers-Wright | 73
    5.2 A Leadership Turmoil (1978–80) | 85
    5.3 The Administration of the Caretaker, Mr. B. A. King (1978–80) | 88

6. The Administration of Rev. Cannon Z. S. F. Smith (1980–98) | 91
    6.1 The Administration of the Rev. Smith (1980–98) | 93

7. The Consequences of War and Pandemics (1991–2021) | 106
    7.1 Civil War in Sierra Leone (1991–2002) | 106
    7.2 Pandemics and Education in Sierra Leone | 113
    7.3 Post-Crises Electronic Readjustments of the Educational Infrastructure | 116

Postscript | 127
Appendix A: West African Methodist Collegiate School Song | 131
Appendix B: [An unedited/original speech] | 138
Appendix C: [An unedited/original speech] | 145
Bibliography | 151
Index | 155

List of Illustrations and Tables

Figure 1.1: The Triangular Trans-Atlantic Slave Trade | 4

Table 2.1: Foundation Students in 1911 Foundation Students (in alphabetical order, 1911) | 18

Archdeacon C. A. E. Macauley, MBE, MA (Oxon) | 19

Rev. Prof. Orishatukeh Faduma, BD, PhD (Yale) | 23

Table 2.2: Foundation Students in 1948 | 34

Figure 3.1: The School's Crest and Motto | 38

Table 3.1: Staff of the WAM Collegiate School (1948–52) | 43

Sir Maurice Dorman, KCMG (1957) | 51

Rev. I. S. T. Fewry, OBE Alumnus and General Superintendent of the WAM Church | 52

Table 3.2: Staff of the WAM Collegiate School in 1964 | 55

J. A. Garber, Esq., MA (Dunelm), LCP | 56

Rev. V. J. Hastings-Spaine, Esq., BA, DipTh | 61

Rev. Dr. W. E. A. Pratt, OBE, MA, DD | 67

Lewellyn Rogers-Wright, BA (Dun.) | 75

Table 5.1: Players of the Commemorative Soccer Competition in Honor of Mr. Smith | 81

Table 5.2 A Cross-section of Teachers at the Collegiate School (1974–77) | 83

Mr. J. R. Thorpe (1916–2012) | 93

List of Illustrations and Tables

Figure 6.1: Certificate/GCE O'Level Results (Percentage of Success, 1970–84) | 96

Table 6.1: Faculty Members 1984/5 and 1985 | 97

President J. S. Momoh, OBE, Alumnus of the WAM Collegiate School | 99

Table 6.2: The 6-3-3-4 System of Education in Sierra Leone | 105

Figure 7.1 COVID-19 Cases and Deaths (April 1, 2020–November 11, 2020) | 115

Figure 7.2: Individuals Using the Internet (Percent of the Population in the United States and Sierra Leone) | 117

Table 7.1: Teaching Service Commission: Radio Teaching Program Schedule, October 2020 | 119-120

Figure 7.3: Access to Electricity (Percent of the Population in the United States and Sierra Leone) | 121

Box 7.1: Energy Projects (2014–18) | 124

Figure 7.4: Average WASSCE grades (2016–18) | 125

List of Principals of the WAM Collegiate School (1911–2021) | 129

Acknowledgements

I AM OBLIGATED TO do justice to all those who have assisted me in one way or another to complete this book, which started as a dissertation in the 1980s. Substantial information within this book came from primary sources that could not have been obtained from alternative sources. Accordingly, I am very grateful to the late Messrs. S. T. Lewis-Nicol, S. B. Moiba, J. R. Thorpe, T. W. Clarkson, and D. C. Thomas. Mr. James Thorpe, President of the Alumni Association in the United Kingdom and alumni associations of the Collegiate School in the United States and the United Kingdom provided material support.

Information within this book was also derived from material information that was liberally provided by the Rev. Z. S. F. Smith and Miss. Webber, who was Secretary of the Parent Teacher Association (PTA) at the time when I was originally putting the dissertation together. The employees of the Filing Section of the Ministry of Education and Information and Mrs. Eliott of the West African Examination Council (WAEC) made it possible for me to have access to government information on the school and other helpful examination data. However, this book would not have been possible without diligent work and the supervision of my dissertation. Inspiration came from some prominent Reverend gentlemen, primarily the late Rev. Emile E. Jones (who was my advisor and Professor of Biblical and Religious Studies at FBC), the Rev. S. P. Jackson, the Rev. J. M. Pratt, and the Rev. Campbell Coker. Invariably, dissertations have to be supervised.

Professor Cyril P. Foray, vice principal of Fourah Bay College (FBC) and Head of the History Department at the time, invested time in reviewing the details of the contents of my dissertation in the 1984/5 academic year. Mr. Emmanuel Larry King, a personal friend, who wrote a dissertation on the

Acknowledgements

Sierra Leone Grammar School, encouraged me to write something about the Collegiate School. His suggestion was obviously fortuitous and rewarding.

The dissertation was compiled and preserved for posterity by a typist because computers were not freely and readily available at the time. The compilation and preservation of information could only facilitate prompt (timely) recapitulation and visualization of original facts or data; for this reason, I am very grateful to Mrs. Seliatu Koroma, who worked for the Demographics Unit at FBC, for memorializing the initial contents of the type-written work. Data were collected for this book, the contents were supervised and reappraised in the 1980s, and inspiration was provided for its expansion. In the final analysis, I take full responsibility for the evolution and contents of this book.

Christopher E. S. Warburton, PhD
February, 2021

Introduction

THIS BOOK IS AN extension of a dissertation in partial fulfillment of the degree of BA (Hons) in History (1985) from Fourah Bay College, the University of Sierra Leone. At the time of its inception, and under the auspices of the Department Chair of History, Mr. C. P. Foray—who was also a Minister of Foreign Affairs of the Sierra Leonean Government from 1969 to 1971—the dissertation chronicled the history of the West African Methodist Collegiate School till 1985. The WAM Collegiate School was one of many secondary schools in Sierra Leone at the time. Therefore, the contemporary form of this book is a reflection of a very robust history of the school in the context of religious and secular historical experiences that transverse more than a century of the school's existence.

Consequently, the book is more than the history of a school. It highlights some of the most transformational experiences in Sierra Leone and how circumstantial changes in the world, dating back to the days of slavery, altered the lives of many in Sierra Leone and Africa. The book chronicles the daring efforts of missionaries to bring education to Sierra Leone, including the various challenges that confronted the endeavors of missionaries as they tried to spread religious and secular education in Sierra Leone. The preponderant contents of the book are unique and unabridged.

Christian education was essential to the dissemination of Christian theology in Sierra Leone and Africa, but education meant much more to the missionaries. Education meant producing clergymen, teachers, doctors, civil servants, lawyers, and judges to serve not only in Freetown but the nooks and crannies of the country. Indeed, missionaries and teachers ventured into the remotest places of Sierra Leone and Africa in order to spread religious and secular education.

Introduction

The spread of Christianity meant establishing schools as a very fundamental foundation. After the emancipation of slaves, it was critically important for former slaves and even recaptives to be educated. In fact, the motives to educate and proselytize were never circumscribed by the circumstances of enslavement. Education was open to all those who had the desire to embrace the Christian vision or values of life.

To accomplish the objectives of the missionaries, several schools were established in Freetown along denominational lines. Interestingly, the formative years were characterized by denominational sensitivities; fierce denominational competition also defined the educational landscape of Freetown. Over time, hypersensitivities were relaxed and strict denominational requirements gave way to tolerant education that coexisted with denominational interests.

Missionary work was conducted in political and social circumstances that helped to configure the choices that were to be made and the methods of delivery of education. Consequently, the history of the Collegiate School cannot be extricated from the broader political and social circumstances in Sierra Leone; the very circumstances that helped to shape the evolution of the school in Freetown. In this book, the history of the school is presented in seven chapters to cover the significant incidents that marked its existence from 1911 to 2021. The incidents shaped the evolution and challenges that confronted the school.

Chapter 1 presents the immediate historical circumstances that prefaced the establishment of the school. A brief historical background of the emancipation and resettlement of slaves is discussed in the chapter. The chapter lays the basis for an understanding of the education of the inhabitants of Freetown and the adjoining areas; more so, it exposes some of the difficulties that were associated with developing alien settlements in Freetown. There was a conspicuous need for missionaries and teachers to make the emancipated slaves and local inhabitants more productive and useful so that they could earn a living and be independently prosperous.

I present the formative years of the school (1911–27) in chapter 2. The school was first established by the United Methodist Free Churches (UMFCs) of England, and the chapter also provides historical context of the UMFCs. The formative years reflect the strict missionary objective of the school in conjunction with the financial challenges that beset the proprietors of the school. Finding teachers and students was a challenging endeavor, but surgical precision was utilized to profile and recruit students

Introduction

with aptitude to perform the missionary work of the denomination. Apparently, the intake of students was not limited to Freetown; over time, more students came from various regions of West Africa. Migration necessitated boarding facilities. The school ran into administrative and financial difficulties and it eventually closed down in 1927, only to be reopened after more than two decades of abeyance.

Chapter 3 is dedicated to the life of the highly improbable school after it was reopened in 1948. The challenges that endangered the continuity of the school (after it reopened) are presented in the chapter. The chapter is illustrative of the foundations of the development of the modern Collegiate School. Pioneering developments discussed in chapter 3 include the determination of the West African Methodist Church to ensure the sustainability of the school. It was during this period that the school's song, motto, and crest, were developed. The architects of the significant developments are acknowledged in the chapter. The formidable existential threats to the school between 1948 and 1962 are also discussed in the chapter.

Chapters 4 through 6 examine changes or improvements that were made to the school under different principals and administrative preferences. There were various curriculum modifications and disciplinary issues. The marching band of the school came into existence in the 1970s after protracted efforts and multiple incidents of embarrassment to provide one.

Financial problems continued to impede the progress of the school after the 1940s, but by the 1960s the restrictive preference of the school was relaxed. More females were admitted into the school as faculty members in the 1970s and the relaxation became a hallmark of gender diversification. The ebb and flow of students created accommodation and structural problems; there were episodic problems with insufficient chairs and desks, leadership turmoil, and explosive discontents.

The final chapter of the book takes a look at contemporary challenges in contradistinction to the conditions that predated the establishment of the school in 1911 and its resuscitation in the 1940s. The concept of education is examined in the context of the consequences of a civil war and pandemics (external threats). These threats highlight the need for technological innovation and more equitable income distribution that can only be provided by deliberate national policies. The consequences of the threats are naturally counterproductive and stifling.

Efforts by the national government to deal with the looming contemporary changes confronting modern educational institutions are discussed

Introduction

in conjunction with collaborative international efforts to make education more accessible and affordable. The history of the WAM Collegiate School is a rich rendition of the coalescence of missionary work, human courage and determination, human failures, ambition, and existential threats that transverse more than a century of the existence of the school. The interface of circumstances and educational outcomes continuously reminds us that more is always desirable and attainable; *Plus Ultra*!

1

Historical Background of the WAM Collegiate School

THE WAM COLLEGIATE SCHOOL is a byproduct of missionary work in West Africa; specifically, Sierra Leone. Like most of the schools that were established in Sierra Leone during the twentieth century, the school has a unique history that is encapsulated by the history of the Colony of Sierra Leone and what is more generally characterized as "Freetown" today. The Sierra Leonean Colony was a geographic entity of dislodged settlers during the waning days of the trans-Atlantic slave trade. Diverse groups of settlers formed a unique culture that was characterized by an intrinsic admixture of indigenous practices and Western values with a deep-seated appreciation of Christianity (after the exposure to Western culture).

From the sixteenth to about the last two decades of the eighteenth century, commercial relations between the Europeans and the Africans on the west coast of Africa were generally centered on the heinous and opprobrious triangular trans-Atlantic trade in slaves (see Figure 2.1).[1] The experience of the slave trade was chaotic and destabilizing, and it fundamentally altered the lives and developmental prospects of many African polities;

---

1. Slaves were transported from the West Coast of Africa—for example, from Nigeria, Sierra Leone, Guinea, and Senegal—to the Caribbean (West Indies) and America (mostly through South Carolina) to grow rice, tobacco, and sugar, in return for guns (firearms) liquor, tobacco, and Western luxuries, which were then transported to Europe. Guns, rum, and luxury goods were then transported to the west coast of Africa for more slaves. The weapons intensified ethno-economic wars to control trade routes and markets, and capture more slaves who were then traded to work on the plantations in the West Indies and America; see also the Gullah people of South Carolina.

for example, Walter Rodney argued that the tremendous reduction in the African population, occasioned by the slave trade, was responsible for the slothful economic development of Africa; partly because the most productive component of the African population was exported from Africa.

However, between the last three decades of the eighteenth century and the first two of the nineteenth century, European attitudes to the slave trade changed for a variety of reasons—including humanitarian and economic—because the trade in humans became a demoded form of economic transaction that could not coexist with new forms of industrialization. Apart from the genuine humanitarian or philanthropic resentment of the slave trade, the uneasy competition between the agrarian and industrial interests of production diminished the predominance of the slave trade as a persistent form of international economic transaction. In the 1770s, the trade in slaves increasingly became odious, and in 1807, the British Parliament declared participation in the trade by British citizens and subjects to be illegal. The termination of the trade was not immediate. In 1772, the abolitionists achieved significant success in the case of James Somerset.[2] The success was essential but insufficient. Even though English law did not formerly recognize slavery, the slave trade continued till its abolition in 1833 and thereafter.

By 1772, there were about 14,000 domestic slaves under the ownership of British farmers who were on leave or retirement in the West Indies.[3] The Mansfield pronouncement implicitly meant that at least 14,000 slaves were to be freed immediately. London became a magnet for former slaves who desired their freedom; slaves feverishly found ways to travel to London in order to be free. Naturally, London became a congested city with ex-slaves who lacked the opportunity and the wherewithal to eke out a living.

---

2. James Somerset was a slave who was transported from Jamaica to England in 1769 by his Bostonian American master, Charles Stewart. He escaped in 1771 but he was recaptured and put on board a ship that was bound for Jamaica, where he was to be sold. Though slaves were considered to be chattels and the transaction was considered to be a normal practice in the eighteenth century, Granville Sharp, a staunch British abolitionist and humanitarian, decided to make a test case of the Somerset situation. Using a writ of habeas corpus, he successfully had Somerset removed from the ship before it could set sail for Jamaica. He did so on the grounds that Somerset's presence in England gave him the status of a free man. A lengthy case ensued, but in 1772, the Lord Chief Justice Mansfield declared that slavery was so odious, even in the absence of a legal precedent and declarative law, that Somerset must be freed. In effect, the Chief Justice used a principle of jurisprudence that was based on equity and fundamental fairness (*ex aequo et bono*). The far reaching and consequential pronouncement meant that Stewart lost his chattel and that slaves who set foot on English soil can be freed.

3. Omer-Cooper et al., *Growth of African Civilization*, 131.

Historical Background of the WAM Collegiate School

Vagabondary, loitering, and begging became a way of life on the streets of London and the ex-slaves became a menace and eyesore to the British and their way of life within a short period of time. The ex-slaves had to be reoriented and resettled but not before their pitiful situation caught the eyes of philanthropists.

Some of the humanitarians developed committees to alleviate the plight of the ex-slaves; for example, "The Committee for the Black Poor," under the Chairmanship of Jonas Hanway, was formed in 1786 to alleviate the suffering of the black poor. The Committee accepted the advice of Mr. Henry Smeathman—who had traveled to Africa—that Sierra Leone would be a suitable environment for the experimental repatriation of the Negroes. The British Government agreed to provide transportation and financial assistance, and a handbill was disseminated inviting acceptance for free passage to Sierra Leone under the auspices of the Committee.[4]

It is estimated that about 500 or 510 passengers embarked in Portsmouth, of which there were about 440 black males and females and about sixty or seventy white males and females.[5] About 377 arrived on May 9, 1787 after the others perished.[6] The prototypical experiment, "Sierra Leone Experiment," which had been pioneered by Granville Sharp, was supposed to be idealistic, democratic, and self-governing. An ancient system of government, known as the "frankpledge," which was practiced in ancient Israel and England at the time of King Alfred, was adopted. People were broken up into tithings (a family of ten) and each tithing elected a leader on an annual basis known as a "Tithingman." Every ten tithingmen then elected a leader, Hundredor, on an annual basis, and together the Hundredors and Tithingmen governed the settlement.[7]

Sharp's "Province of Freedom" did not work out smoothly as expected. The rainy season, inadequate shelter, disease (emanating from adverse

---

4. Porter, *Creoledom*, 20.

5. Porter, *Creoledom*, 20.

6. There are conflictive reports about the attributes of the Negro passengers. Granville Sharp reports that they were mostly Seamen that had served in the Royal Navy or as Rangers with the Army in the American Woods. Later reports postulated that they were all men who had been discharged from the army and navy after the American War, or slaves who had been transported to England by their masters. The earliest information about the white women came from Mrs. Anna Maria Falconbridge who wrote that they mostly walked the streets of London and supported themselves by prostitution (Porter, *Creoledom*, 21).

7. Foray, *Historical Dictionary of Sierra Leone*, xxxvii.

weather conditions), and hostilities with the neighboring tribes—who had sold the Sierra Leonean Peninsula to the Black Poor Committee—decimated the early settlers.[8] An indignant subchief subsequently burnt down the early settlement and the settlers dispersed. Sharp's Province of Freedom succumbed to hostilities and destruction. Yet the humanitarians were determined to restore the settlement and improve the lives of the poor.

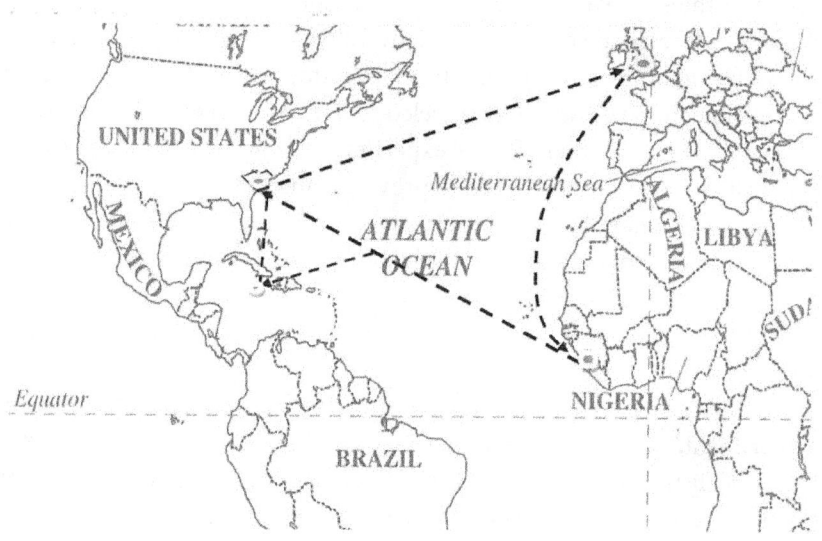

Figure 1.1: The Triangular Trans-Atlantic Slave Trade

The St. George's Bay Company, which had been constituted in 1790 to facilitate more "honorable trade with the coast of Africa," soon became a valuable reference point for the reconstitution of the settlement in Sierra Leone. In 1791, the St. George's Bay Company sent out Dr. Falconbridge (as an agent of the company) to examine and report on the state of the Colony and to provide temporary relief to its settlers until a charter could be obtained that would have enabled the directors to take more affirmative and permanent measures to ensure the prosperity of settlement.[9]

---

8. It is unclear whether the terms of the sale of land were well-understood and generally affirmed. The traditional but anachronistic practice of communal ownership of land is still prevalent and recognized in certain parts of the country at the time of this writing. The treaty with Temne chiefs had granted about ten miles of land along the coast of Freetown for £60 worth of goods, largely in the forms of rum, tobacco, arms, and ammunition.

9. Porter, *Creoledom*, 23.

Historical Background of the WAM Collegiate School

The demise of the Province of Freedom revealed that transplanting ex-slaves and indigent people from Europe to Africa was an unusual experiment with costly consequences. Later in 1791, the St. George's Bay Company received a new charter and the company was subsequently transformed into a powerful and financially viable company known as the "Sierra Leone Company." The financial clout made it possible to undertake new settlements that could be financially supported in Sierra Leone. Therefore, the prospects and fortunes of settlements in Sierra Leone were elevated in 1792. In January of 1792, about 1,200 freed slaves arrived in Sierra Leone from Nova Scotia.[10]

The Nova Scotians had a relatively elevated or sophisticated lifestyle because of their exposure to diasporan life.[11] Liberated Africans (Recaptives) never made the voyage across the Atlantic before they were recaptured on the high seas and sent back to Africa. They naturally had a different level of sophistication, which made them susceptible to discrimination because of their perceived cultural inferiority; they were considered to be "Recaptives." As the more sophisticated settlers intermarried with the Recaptives to form a distinct group of settlers known as the *Krios* or *Creoles*, the dichotomous status distinction subsequently morphed into status crystallization. *Krios and Creoles* are often used interchangeably without necessarily separating the people from the language, which is an admixture of a corruption of the English and indigenous languages (*Pidgin English or Patois*).[12] *Krio* is more often used to describe the language.

In actual fact, the financial problems of the private companies that embarked on the audacious enterprise of resettling people in Africa were rather refractory. As a result, funds became perennially inadequate and the relationship between the settlers and the company contentiously deteriorated as more settlers loitered the streets of Freetown. Within the first decade of the nineteenth century the population of the Colony had increased, consisting

---

10. Foray, *Historical Dictionary of Sierra Leone*, xxxviii.

11. The Nova Scotians of Sierra Leone were considered to be Loyalists Negroes who had fought alongside the British in America during the American War of Independence. They consisted of freedmen and slaves who were resettled in Nova Scotia, a province of Canada, before being transported to Freetown. One of their numbers, Thomas Peters, had traveled to London to petition the financially viable Sierra Leone Company (formerly the St. George's Bay Company) to transplant the Negroes from the harsh climatic conditions of Nova Scotia to a more natural and warmer environment. His voyage coincided with discussions of trade and resettlement in Freetown; see Porter, *Creoledom*, 23–25.

12. Fyle, *Historical Dictionary of Sierra Leone*, and Porter, *Creoledom*, for further reading about the Krios.

of survivors of the original settlement, the Nova Scotians, Maroons, Recaptives, and tribal immigrants who had migrated from adjacent lands.

The company ultimately decided to levy quit rent as a source of income to finance its operations. The company had decided that no quit rent on land will be paid till the midsummer of 1792, after which quit rent (tax) of no more than one shilling an acre will be levied for two years on a semiannual basis; thereafter, it was expected to be increased to 2 percent on the gross produce of the land.[13] Between 1794 and 1801, quit rents became the most contentious source of friction between the company and the settlers. Rather than pay the rents, some settlers abandoned designated lands to seek habitation and livelihood elsewhere. The hateful rents were perceived as coercively violative of the freedoms that the settlers had enjoyed under Granville Sharp's Province of Freedom. Hostility to the quit rents led to their abolition in 1803, though the policy episodically surfaced till 1832.

From 1800 and thereabout, the British Parliament voted annual subsidies as grants-in-aid for the Colony's civil establishment and defence[14] However, financial challenges and external threats made it extremely difficult for the company to manage the settlement; even with its laudable goal of ending slavery and embarking on a civilizing mission.[15] The overwhelming problems and financial challenges confronting the company eventually caused the company to cede its political functions to the British Crown. On January 1, 1808, Sierra Leone became a Crown Colony after the cessation of the political functions of the company.

In arbitrating the competing theories for the abolition of slavery, historians have advanced various theories under the bifurcated categories of humanitarian and economic; for example, Coupland, Mathieson, and Mellor emphasized the humanitarian endeavor. Williams presented a countervailing economic view with a Marxist twist. Nevertheless, it can hardly be a convincing proposition that there was a singular and persuasive driver behind the movement to abolish the slave trade.

The interaction of humanitarian and economic motives to end slavery, coupled with unparalleled human initiative to transform the lives of former slaves, provide a realistic compromise of equanimity. More so, it

---

13. Foray, *Historical Dictionary of Sierra Leone*, 179.

14. Foray, *Historical Dictionary of Sierra Leone*, xxxix.

15. Apart from domestic fissures, tensions in Europe reached the West African shores of Sierra Leone; for example, as hostilities developed between the British and the French, French naval squadrons attacked the Freetown settlement in 1794.

seems to me that the passionate resolve and consequential intervention of the humanitarians and philanthropists can hardly be trivialized or made subsidiary to the herculean and dispositive efforts to terminate the inhumane trade in slaves. In actual fact, the competing theories were rather estranged from the indigent situation of the ex-slaves, which caught the attention of the humanitarians. Further, the work of the humanitarians and philanthropists transcended the termination of the slave trade. How could the slaves who had been deprived of human capital be functionally relevant to their societies? Where should the emancipated slaves be settled? What should be the post-slavery mode of life? The questions coalesced around the development of pedagogical institutions in Sierra Leone, especially the Colony of Sierra Leone.

The British Government was incapable of providing and financing all the essential services of its colonies all over the world. Missionary work augmented the scope of such a colossal financial undertaking. As such, the religious order was critical in rehabilitating former slaves and creating avenues for the development of enviable human capital that first benefited the Creoles and later the indigenes of Sierra Leone who were derisively considered to be rustic by western standards. The subsequent dispersal of settlers made the administration and provision of services much more demanding.

The Recaptives, a later group of settlers, built huts in mountainous villages, possibly as a protective and defensive measure against external aggression. Cabenda (later named as "Wilberforce" by Sir Charles MacCarthy in 1816) was established by an Acting Governor, Lt. R. Bones, as the new home for forty-two Recaptives from an estuary of the Congo, Cabenda. In 1827, some Recaptives settled in Pa Sandi Village (later renamed "Lumley" after the acting governor, Lt-Col Lumley, who resettled them in that location in 1827). With the aid of Governor MacCarthy, others were settled in Hogbrook (renamed "Regent") and ten more villages in the Colony in 1820.[16] The villages had to be serviced by educational resources and the missionaries filled that void. Though some have characterized the missionaries as the ideological wing of Western capitalism, there is every reason to believe that some of the missionaries must have genuinely felt the need to disseminate Christian education with theological or religious fervor.

The missionaries became responsible for several schools in the villages. Sumner (1963) observed that:

---

16. Foray, *Historical Dictionary of Sierra Leone*, 126.

Up to 1900, there were three secondary schools for boys and three for girls. The boys' secondary schools were: (1) Sierra Leone Grammar School founded by the Church Missionary Society [C.M.S.] in 1845; (2) Wesleyan Boys' High School founded by the Wesleyan Methodist Church in 1874; (3) Leopold Educational Institute, founded by the Rev. L.J. Leopold in 1884. The girls' secondary schools: (1) Annie Walsh Memorial School founded by the C.M.S. in 1845; (2) Wesleyan Girls' High School opened in 1880 by the Wesleyan Methodist connexion; (3) St. Joseph's Convent, begun as a primary school in 1866. From 1900 to 1916 the following additional secondary schools were opened: (1) Albert Academy, founded by the United Brethren in Christ Mission in 1904; (2) A.M.E. Seminary opened by the American Methodist Episcopal Church in 1908; (3) United Methodist Collegiate [later the W.A.M. Collegiate] School founded by the United Methodist Free Church in 1911.[17]

The preconditions for the evolution of pedagogical instruction in Freetown were fortuitously provided by Governor MacCarthy (the governor of Sierra Leone from 1814 to 1824). Prior to the advent of the governor, Gen. Sir Charles MacCarthy, the relationship between governors and the governed had strenuously strayed in Sierra Leone. MacCarthy ushered in a period of nineteenth-century reconstruction for Sierra Leone. He saw the problem of resettlement not in terms of profit maximization but as a matter of administrative and humanitarian reconstruction.

The governor devised a scheme for reorganizing the liberated Africans (Recaptives) into Christian communities and vigorously pursued funds from the British treasury. He forged alliances between the British Government and the Church Missionary Society (CMS) so that the church can provide the personnel for clergy work and teaching. The governor divided the colony into thirteen parishes, which were supervised by CMS clergymen who were paid by the government.[18] Pressured by the governor to provide funds or subsidy, the British Government provided funds for churches, schools, and personages. The governor also introduced several reforms to break down racial barriers and increase settler participation in the governance of their affairs. Foray writes:

> In terms of length of tenure, in terms of promoting the welfare of the Recaptives, in terms of establishing cordial relationships

---

17. Sumner, *Education in Sierra Leone*, 150.
18. Foray, *Historical Dictionary of Sierra Leone*, 125.

Historical Background of the WAM Collegiate School

between government and the governed, his governorship, if somewhat extravagant in expenditure and visionary in some of its aims, was second to none in 19th-century Sierra Leone.[19]

The next chapter will take a look at missionary work and the formative years of the Collegiate School.

---

19. Foray, *Historical Dictionary of Sierra Leone*, 126.

2

The Formative Years of the Collegiate School (1911–27)

NEITHER THE BRITISH GOVERNMENT nor the missionaries were willing to carry out the ambitious proposals of Governor MacCarthy. However, the missionaries adopted comparable measures for the rehabilitation of the Recaptives. Churches and schools were built in the villages that were set up by the governor, and in Freetown. For the most part, the missionaries provided the personnel for operating the churches and schools; a gesture that was extended into the twentieth century. The African Institution, the Wesleyan Methodist Missionary Society, the CMS, the Countess of Huntingdon Connexion, the West African Methodist Society, and the United Methodist Free Churches (UMFCs) became pioneers of the construction of schools and the expansion of Western education. The UMFCs were particularly instrumental in the establishment of the United Methodist (UM) Collegiate School.

2.1 The United Methodist Free Churches

As the missionaries competed to make quality education available to residents of the Colony, pedagogy and denominational competition became rife in Freetown. Some denominations were clearly able to outperform others in the feverish rush to spread education in the Colony; for example, while the WAMS could boast of four schools by 1852, the UMFCs of England had

The Formative Years of the Collegiate School (1911–27)

control over ten schools in Sierra Leone by 1863[1] and the Collegiate School was added to the growing number in 1911.

In the later part of the nineteenth century, the UMFCs of England, also referred to as the Free Methodists, were considered to be nonconformists because they did not conform to the rules and authority of the Church of England. They were an amalgamation of churches that came together in 1857. The combination consisted of the Wesleyan Association and the Wesleyan Reformers.[2] The UMFCs subsequently merged with the Bible Christian Church and the Methodist New Connexion to form the United Methodist Church in 1907. The UMFCs were known to have sent missionaries to various colonies, including Australia. Merging with four other Methodist denominations, the UMFCs reconstituted itself into the Methodist Church of Australasia in 1902.[3]

The behavior in some of the churches in Freetown was less than holistic. Subdued feelings of superiority and inferiority characterized the relationship between the Nova Scotians and the Recaptives in places of worship. The Recaptive preachers were not given the same privileges as the Nova Scotian preachers though they had amassed sufficient education to speak intelligently and articulate the Christian doctrine. Recaptive preachers were not permitted to ascend the pulpit of West African Churches. Rev. Joseph Janet, a Nova Scotian preacher, had generated a large following of Recaptives, but he would neither ordain Recaptives to be preachers nor allow them to ascend the pulpit (what the Recaptives considered to be the "Big Pulpit").

In 1833, rebellion broke out in the church as one of the Recaptive preachers of Porpor descent, Anthony O'Connor, who was converted at a Rawdon Street Chapel, decided not to submit to degradation anymore but to form a Church for the Recaptives, the West African Methodist Society (WAMS), which was also called the "African Church" in 1844.[4] Clearly, the social stereotypes of superordination and subordination had fizzled, at least in the minds of the Recaptives, during the twentieth century.

1. Sumner, *Education in Sierra Leone*, 76.

2. The Wesleyan Association absorbed the Protestant Methodist (1828) in 1836. The Wesleyan Reformers were Wesleyan Methodists who were expelled for insubordination in 1849.

3. Another major Methodist branch was the United Methodist Church, which emerged from earlier mergers of smaller Methodist groupings. The UMC joined with other Methodists and Wesleyan Methodists in 1932 to form the Methodist Church in Britain.

4. Shodekeh-Johnson, "Growth and Development," 4.

The West African Methodist Collegiate School, 1911–2021

Implicit in the breakup were educational challenges; the manpower to conduct missionary activities.

Realizing that the WAMS needed moral and financial support, the Superintendent of the Huntingdon Connexion, the Rev. Trotter, suggested that the leaders of the WAMS approach the UMFCs of England. The WAMS and the UMFCs had synergistic rules. In 1858, the Rev. Trotter initiated contact by mail with the Rev. Eckett in London to facilitate an admission of the WAMS into the UMFCs. In 1859, the WAMS applied for admission into the UMFCs through the Conference in England.

On April 19, 1859, the UMFCs accepted the proposal for an amalgamation of the WAMS and the UMFCs. The UMFCs were thus inclined to send missionaries to assist the teething WAMS. For a start, the UMFCs sent a single minister, the Rev. Joseph New. In response to the letter of the WAMS, an optimistic note of further cooperation was struck: "members will be increased and many influential persons will become members of our Connexion."[5]

The church experienced some setbacks[6] but cooperation between the WAMS and the UMFCs thrived and two more European Methodist denominations joined the union in 1907. The conglomerate communities adopted a new name, the United Methodist Church (UMC) to reflect the new status of amalgamation.

Fully aware of the need to educate the African Methodist children to become clergymen, teachers, and skilled workers in the Colony and Protectorate, another appeal was made by the Africans to the UMFCs for additional financial and moral support. The UMFCs responded favorably and the General Superintendent of the Church in Freetown, the Rev. Greensmith, together with members of the denomination, decided to establish a missionary (parochial) school for the education of boys who were affiliated with the Connexion. The institution that was established on June 1, 1911, became known as the "United Methodist (UM) Collegiate School," partly because of its affiliation with the UMFCs of England. The birth of the Collegiate School was incremental and tortuous, and it was evidently established as a sectarian (Methodist) and non-coeducational institution (not for boys and girls).

---

5. Shodekeh-Johnson, "Growth and Development," 9.

6. As a result of unfavorable weather conditions, the Rev. New succumbed to death in 1862. After arriving in Freetown on 10 June, 1859, Rev. Warboys (who succeeded the Rev. New as Superintendent) also died shortly thereafter. The Rev. James Browne served in their capacity from 1862 to 1864.

The Formative Years of the Collegiate School (1911–27)

2.2 The School and the First Principals (1911–27)

The dreams of the members of the UMC branch in Freetown came to fruition when they opened the UMC Collegiate School. The members of the UMC branch in Freetown fitted a tentative structure at number 8 Pademba Road to commence the operations of the school and the attic was used as a dwelling place for the principal. The lower portion of the building was used to conduct classes. A second building, which faced Soldier Street, was used to house students from the Protectorate and other areas of Africa.[7] A large passage connected the two buildings. Two rooms of the Soldier Street building were converted into classrooms as enrolment increased.

An impressive inaugural service was held in Samaria Church to commemorate the founding or establishment of the school. In a show of solidarity, the service was attended by ministers and representative members of churches in other denominations in and out of Freetown. The General Superintendent, the Rev. Greensmith, gave a short address that was reminiscent of the history of the school. At the end of the service, the members and congregation engaged in an impromptu procession, marching along Westmoreland Street, turning the corner of Percival Street, and wending their way to number 8 Pademba Road.[8] The celebratory march has been an ongoing tradition ever since, albeit with planning and anticipatory splendor.

At the outset, the school was able to recruit Archdeacon C. A. E. Macauley, BA (Oxford) as principal; Mr. B. E. Cummings, BA; Johnny W. Wallace, BA; O'Neil M. Renner, BA; and J. D. Williams as some of its teachers.[9] On Friday June 1, 1911, the school day ended after enrollment and classes started in earnest the following day (Saturday, June 2, 1911) at 7:30 AM.

The first principal of the school, Christian Athanasius Evrett Macauley, was born in Freetown in 1880. He was the last of the six children of Mr. and Mrs. Charles and Selina Macauley.[10] He was educated at the Educational Institute (commonly known as the Leopold School) and the CMS Grammar School. After completing secondary education, he worked for the Customs Department while simultaneously studying to become an official of the

---

7. The Protectorate was the larger area of Sierra Leonean land, which came under British Protection in 1896. The Colony, in contradistinction to the Protectorate, was the portion of Sierra Leonean land that the British Crown acquired by cession, annexation, or treaty in 1807.

8. See *The Sierra Leone Weekly News*, 1 July, 1911, p. 5.

9. Pratt, *Autobiography*, 10.

10. See *Collegiate School Diamond Jubilee Handbook 1911–1971*, 14.

church. He was subsequently financed by the UMFCs to study at Ranmoor College in England to prepare for missionary work. After three years, he completed his education at Ranmoor College. Instead of returning to Freetown, he proceeded to Oxford University for a bachelor's degree. After successfully completing the bachelor's degree, he pursued a master's degree and became the first Sierra Leonean to graduate from Oxford.[11] After eight years in London, he returned home and the UMC saw an opportunity to recruit him as the first principal of the UMC Collegiate School; a position he held till 1915. He was succeeded by the Rev. Prof. Orishatukeh Faduma.

Professor Faduma, who is of Yoruba descent, was born on September 15, 1857 in Demerara, British Guyana, as William J. Davis. His parents (John and Omolofi Davis) were victims of the disruptive trans-Atlantic slave trade. On their way to slavery in the Indies, they were rescued by a British anti-slavery squadron in the mid-Atlantic and taken to British Guyana—instead of resettlement in Sierra Leone—to work on the Colony's coffee and sugar plantations.[12] Professor Faduma's parents became Christians and adopted the family name, Davis (in honor of a Welsh missionary), before Professor Faduma was born.

The Davis family eventually migrated to Africa and settled in the village of Waterloo, which was founded in 1819, in Sierra Leone. Professor Faduma eventually had missionary [Wesleyan] education in the village of Waterloo. At the age of nineteen, in 1876, "John," as he was called, moved from Waterloo to Freetown, where he stayed with the founder and principal of the Wesleyan Boys High School in Freetown, Mr. J. C. May. Prof. Faduma later became a teacher at the Wesleyan Boys High School as both a Junior and Senior Master. He subsequently earned a scholarship to study at Queen's College in Taunton, England, from 1882 to 1883. After Queen's College, he attended the University of London, where he became the first West African to obtain an Intermediate BA from London University in 1885.[13]

After completing his studies in England, Professor Faduma returned to Freetown in 1885 and, as a tribute to his deep sense of loyalty to his cultural heritage, officially adopted the name Orishatukeh Faduma on 5 August, 1887. The action was a revolutionary undertaking in that he became the

11. *Collegiate School Diamond Jubilee Handbook 1911–1971*, 14.

12. See Simeon; see also Moore. Slavery generated internal strife and wars in most of Africa. The wars were usually for control of trade routes and captives of war to be sold as slaves for rum, tobacco, and ammunition. The Yoruba land was no exception to the turbulence that emanated from the slave trade.

13. Okonkwo, "Orishatukeh Faduma," 24.

The Formative Years of the Collegiate School (1911–27)

first Liberated African to adopt a name as a symbol of protest against names with no inherent or indigenous cultural affiliation with the African culture. Notably, he returned to Freetown with a conspicuous appreciation for African culture and growing dissatisfaction with perceived corruptive European influences on West African culture. On his return, he also taught at the Wesleyan Boys High School, where he distinguished himself as a teacher and community leader. Professor Faduma was an ardent Pan-Africanist and a strong supporter of the Dress Reform Society (DRS) in Freetown, which was established in 1887.[14] Evidently, he aspired to higher heights.

In 1890, he left Freetown for the United States (US, Philadelphia) in search of better opportunities and a career. He was first employed as a teacher by the African Methodist Episcopal Church in Philadelphia. He later moved south to another African Methodist Church-supported school, the Kittrell Normal and Industrial Institute in Kittrell, North Carolina, where he taught for several years and became principal in 1891.

Professor Faduma's avid interest in liberal theology led him to enroll in the Yale Divinity School in September of 1891. After graduation from the Divinity School with a BD in 1894, he spent an additional year at Yale University to study the philosophy of religion and Semitic languages. On May 9, 1895, he was ordained as a Congregational Minister.[15] He was then appointed superintendent of the Peabody Academy as well as pastor of the Congregational Church in Troy, North Carolina, where he worked with his wife until 1914. He resided in the all-black town of Boley, Oklahoma, for a few months, and got involved with the back-to-Africa movement.[16] Pro-

---

14. The DRS was an outward manifestation of a new ethnic consciousness, which swept through Freetown in the 1880s. The members adopted dresses—loose flowing garments—to highlight their separate racial identity; see Foray, *Historical Dictionary of Sierra Leone*, 62; see also Fyle, *Historical Dictionary of Sierra Leone*, 42. The new approach was designed to retire the preference for Victorian attire that was very popular among the Creoles—the Religion of the Frock Coat and Tall (Top) Hat—which many Creoles associated with the attainment of Christianity and civilization; see Simeon. In December 1887, in a meeting of the DRS, Faduma modeled a prospective loose-fitting tunic and gown won over the knee breeches that were expected to be a unique Sierra Leonean attire to replace the European and Victorian model.

15. Okonkwo, "Orishatukeh Faduma," 26. He married a graduate of Atlanta University's Normal School for Teachers, Henrietta Rebecca Adams (1865–1948), in 1896, with whom he subsequently had two children.

16. He worked with one of the visible entities, Akim Trading Company, which pioneered the movement.

fessor Faduma returned to Sierra Leone to serve as principal of the UMC Collegiate School in Freetown from 1916 to 1918.

Professor Faduma was succeeded by the Rev. J. M. Asapansa Johnson, MA, ACP. The Rev. Josephus Milton Asapansa Johnson was born in Freetown in 1890, and he was the son of an exemplary school teacher, Mr. G. A. Johnson, commonly known as "Kobina Johnson."[17] Mr. G. A. Johnson taught his son, Rev. Asapansa Johnson, at Bathurst Street Day School, where the Rev. Asapansa Johnson obtained his primary education. After obtaining secondary education at the Wesleyan Boys High School, the Rev. Asapansa Johnson later proceeded to Fourah Bay College (FBC) of the University of Sierra Leone to obtain bachelor's and master's degrees.[18] He subsequently returned to his alma mater, the Wesleyan Boys High School, to teach for a short period before joining the Staff of the UM Collegiate School to become a Senior Tutor. He was subsequently promoted to the position of vice principal before his appointment as principal of the UM Collegiate School in 1923. His tenure ended when the school closed down in 1927.[19]

2.3 The Administration

The UMC branch in Freetown had hoped that the UMC in England would send a principal to administer the school so that the UMCs of England will have a significant stake in the operation of the school. The Freetown branch wanted to unequivocally enlist the sympathies of the UMCs in England.[20] When the request did not materialize, the UMC of Freetown appointed Archdeacon C. A. E. Macauley to oversee the administration of the school. With inadequate funds to run the affairs of the school, the principal was

---

17. See *Collegiate School Diamond Jubilee Handbook 1911–1971*, 19.

18. *Collegiate School Diamond Jubilee Handbook 1911–1971*, 19.

19. He subsequently went to the United States, became pastor of Allen Memorial Church in Brooklyn, and later, the Bethel Community Church, Staten Island. He was consecrated Bishop of the Old Roman Catholic Church in Chicago in 1964. Mayor William O'Dwyer appointed him to the Mayor's Committee on Unity. He was elected to the Urban League of Greater New York and served as President of the Interdenominational Ministers of Greater New York, which is the oldest association of African-American ministers in the East. He became very active in matters of racial justice but died in Staten Island, New York, on 16 January, 1972.

20. See *The Sierra Leone Weekly News*, 1 July, 1911, p. 5.

The Formative Years of the Collegiate School (1911–27)

paid a monthly salary of five pounds, sixteen shillings, and eight pence (£5.16s.8d.).[21]

Accustomed to the administrative policies of the CMS Grammar School, most of Principal Macauley's policies mirrored that of the CMS Grammar School; for example, students were required to attend classes on Saturdays and classes started very early (at 7:30 AM). Lunch was served at 10:30 AM, classes resumed at 12:30 PM, and the school day ended at 3 PM. However, classes ended at 11 AM on Saturdays.[22]

Since it was the prerogative and mission of the school to educate boys of the UMC denomination, only students of the UMC denomination were admitted into the school during the formative years of the school. The Board of Governors (BoGs) ultimately made the determination as to who will be admitted into the school. The BoGs went in search of foundation students—who were affiliated with the UMC Connexion in Freetown—to be educated as "mission students" after passing a Selective Examination. It was the policy of the Board that one student must be accepted from each of the six circuits; viz: York, Wilberforce, Banana, North, South, and Waterloo Circuits.

Three students attempted the Selective Examination from the York Circuit, Moses C. Pratt, Isaac S. T. Fewry, and W. E. A. Pratt. The successful student was Isaac S. T. Fewry, who later became General Superintendent of the West African Methodist (WAM) Church. Students from other circuits included: E. A. E Cole, from Wilberforce; T. J. V. Campbell, from Banana; T. J. Bright-Leigh, from North; C. M. A. Rollings, from South; and Andrew Palmer, from Waterloo.[23] However, when the school started its operations there were eight foundation students, implying that two students, Franklyn A. Ajaye, and J. B. Fashole-Luke (who enrolled as number 1) were added to the successful entrants from the circuits.

---

21. See *The Collegiate School Diamond Jubilee Handbook 1911–1971*, 75.
22. Pratt, *Autobiography*, 9.
23. Pratt, *Autobiography*, 5.

The West African Methodist Collegiate School, 1911–2021

Table 2.1: Foundation Students in 1911
Foundation Students (in alphabetical order, 1911)

Name	Circuit	Name	Circuit
Ajaye, F. A.	N/A	Fashole-Luke, J. B.	N/A
Bright-Leigh, T. J.	North	Fewry, I. S. T.	York
Cole, E. A. E.	Wilberforce	Palmer, A.	Waterloo
Campbell, T. J. V.	Banana	Rollings, C. M. A.	South

It should not be misconstrued, though, that the admission policy of the BoGs was solely to accept UMC-affiliated residents of the Colony. The BoGs also admitted UMC-affiliated students from the Protectorate and residents of foreign countries. This gesture became more apparent in 1916.

Between 1911 and 1915, student enrolment considerably increased. The school enrolled students who later became prominent political leaders and clergymen: L. F. Luke, I. T. A. Wallace-Johnson (who became a prominent politician), H. E. A. Johnson, D. A. John, L. Bunji Thomas, and W. E. A. Pratt, who later became Chairman and General Superintendent of the Methodist Church in Sierra Leone.

Principal Macauley believed in high moral and academic standards that were equivalent to that of Fourah Bay College (FBC) of the University of Sierra Leone. Therefore, he impressed on students the awareness that secondary education was merely a gateway to the rigors and challenges of tertiary education. Accordingly, the Collegiate School was conceived as a gateway to college education and students were asked to put on a gown and miter.[24] The academic regalia were implicitly symbolic of high educational aspirations and expectations.

The curriculum was structured around three categories—junior, intermediate, and senior.[25] In the first tier of the senior division, students started to prepare for the FBC matriculation examination or the Cambridge Senior Certificate Examination.[26] The school had two terms and promotion was

---

24. Interviews (1984/5) conducted with T. W. Clarkson, F. Thomas, and the Rev. J. A. D. Davies (alumni).

25. Pratt, *Autobiography*, 7.

26. Pratt, *Autobiography*, 10.

The Formative Years of the Collegiate School (1911–27)

done on a terminal rather than annual basis. The first term started in January and ended in August, and the second term proceeded from September to December. Examinations were conducted at the end of each term and promotions were affected accordingly. Prominent courses included arithmetic, Scriptures (later, Bible Knowledge), Latin, algebra, geometry, bookkeeping, English language, French, science, English literature, and music. Saturdays were particularly set aside for music, inter alia.[27]

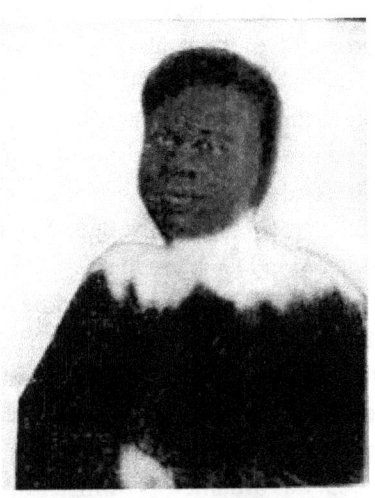

Archdeacon C. A. E. Macauley, MBE, MA (Oxon)
First Principal of the Collegiate School (1911–15)

In 1913, the school had a "Speech Day Ceremony," which is usually an occasion for the principal to address the school and the public. The ceremony was conducted at Wilberforce Memorial Hall, since number 8 Pademba Road had limited capacity and was unsuitable for such an event. A long-lasting ritual was attached to the occasion. As part of the ceremony, pennies (now cents) were distributed. The occasion was subsequently dubbed "Penny Day," albeit under what seems to be different circumstances at a later time. The distribution of coins was a practice that was not peculiar to the Collegiate School because it was also carried out at the CMS Grammar School; therefore, the practice was consistent with the administrative philosophy of harmonization.

---

27. Interviews (1984/5) conducted with T. W. Clarkson and the Rev. J. A. D. Davies (alumni).

The West African Methodist Collegiate School, 1911–2021

The prototypical ceremony was also intended to motivate learning for rewards. Students who worked exceptionally hard were rewarded. Students who demonstrated excellence in their academic work were awarded prizes, usually in the form of books. Students with exceptional records of discipline were awarded monetary prizes by the principal.[28] Qualifications for awards were bifurcated. Students determined qualifications for academic excellence but the principal made decisions about the merits of good behavior.

Financing parochial schools was very challenging. For obvious reasons, the then-government did not assume full financial responsibility for the maintenance of the school. The BoGs and the principal naturally faced serious financial difficulties. Further, the UMCs in England had not unequivocally provided the commitment that was initially expected. Confronting very difficult conditions, mismanagement, and lack of cooperation from the BoGs, Principal Macauley resigned in 1916 for a much more lucrative job in the Education Department.[29]

The leadership vacuum was problematic. The church could not find a ready, suitable, and qualified replacement to manage the affairs of the school with undivided attention. Nevertheless, the members of the church persisted to find a replacement. The church appointed one of its members, the Rev. John Brown Nicols, to act as principal.

The Rev. J. B. Nicols was ordained as Minister of the UMFCs in 1893.[30] Envisaging the need for a well-trained ministry between 1886 and 1887, the Foreign Missions Committee of the UMFCs, in conjunction with the native leaders of the West African Methodists, had appointed the Rev. J. B. Nicols and E. D. L. Thompson to undergo theological training in England. The Rev. Nicols served in various circuits (in Sierra Leone) of the UMFCs and UMCs after his return from training in England.

After 1916, enrolment in the Collegiate School continued to increase to include Ghanaians, Nigerians, Gambians, and students from the Sierra Leonean Protectorate. Additionally, there was a spike in the number of students who transferred from the CMS Grammar School to the UM Collegiate School. At the time, there was growing discontent in the CMS

---

28. Pratt, *Autobiography*, 8.

29. *The Sierra Leone Weekly News*, 8 April, 1916, p. 6. He served as Inspector of Schools at the Education Department until he retired. He later went to the Church of England and rose to the position of Archdeacon. He subsequently served in the Gambia and Conakry, Guinea, where he died on May 5, 1964.

30. *Collegiate School Diamond Jubilee Handbook 1911–1971*, 17.

The Formative Years of the Collegiate School (1911–27)

Grammar School and it is implicit that the strict denominational requirements for admission into the UM Collegiate School had been relaxed.

The crisis in the CMS Grammar School, under the leadership of the Rev. Henry Dallimore, had culminated in strike action and expulsion of students. The grievances of the CMS Grammar School students were imprecisely concrete and specific. Musical instruments of the Grammar School band had disappeared and instruments in the science laboratory could not be accounted for. The science department was closed down, which enraged the students because it seemed as if the principal had not exercised appropriate custodial care over the instruments.[31]

The Borders were also opposed to some of the rules that were imposed by the principal. One of their colleagues, Doherty, had been suspended for failing to work in the fields.[32] With underlying grievances and solidarity with one of their colleagues, the students rebelled and went on strike in May 1915; more pointedly, in remonstration against sloppy administration and what were perceived to be harsh and punitive rules. Student enrollment in Collegiate continued to increase after the strike. Students like Alfred J. Shorenkeh Sawyer, Waribo Cookey, Daniel Carboo, and Sigismund Stowe (all of whom were from Nigeria), and Cyril Koto Richards (from the Gambia) joined the UM Collegiate School.

The Rev. J. B. Nicols was able to stabilize the UM Collegiate School during the turbulent period. However, the UMC members had been actively looking for a principal for the Collegiate School. The arrival of Professor Faduma in Freetown was rather fortuitous and the circumstance gave the UMC members an opportunity to fill the void. Curiously, the Professor was not very enthused about the offer.[33] After some persistence and persuasion, Professor Faduma accepted the offer to be principal of the UM Collegiate School. With a BD and PhD from Yale, Professor Faduma was eminently qualified for the position.

Professor Faduma was instrumental in diversifying and shaping the curriculum of the school after 1916. He brought experiences that he had collected from the academic institutions of the United States to diversify the prototypical emphasis on missionary education. During a Congress on Africa in December of 1895 in Atlanta, Georgia, in the United States, Professor Faduma had strongly argued in favor of the study of African ancestral

---

31. King, "History of the Sierra Leone Grammar School," 62.
32. King, "History of the Sierra Leone Grammar School," 62.
33. King, "History of the Sierra Leone Grammar School," 15.

religions. In effect, he highlighted the importance of studying comparative religion and the philosophy of religion. He introduced the study of vernacular languages, Arabic, Negro history, and African folklore to the Collegiate School as a measure of the diversity of instruction and critical thinking.[34] Most of Professor Faduma's life was spent in the classroom, with a very strong advice to people of African descent that they should take the best of European civilization and reject what is worthless. The Professor stressed the importance of studying things in the African environment and emphasized the importance of African geography and history, customs and industries, and plants and animals, before excursions into those of Europe.

Professor Faduma linked the local dialect to academic instruction. He opined that textbooks should be in local languages for mastery of subject matter in the context of cultural awareness. He reasoned that the native loses his soul when he loses his own language.[35] The Afrocentric emphasis on learning was extended to interpretations of European classics and world civilizations. Professor Faduma urged the translation of the great Western classics into vernacular languages and unwaveringly supported the education of African masses. He called for free and compulsory education for everyone in order to achieve equality of opportunity and movement to status crystallization.[36]

---

34. He served as Inspector and Officer in the Department of Education of Model Schools in Sierra Leone from 1918 to 1923, before returning to the United States to teach Latin, ancient and modern history, and English literature at Lincoln Academy in King's Mount, North Carolina, from 1924 to 1934. In 1927, he enrolled in the summer session of the Chicago Theological Seminary, an affiliate of the University of Chicago's Divinity School. Professor Faduma also taught Latin, Greek, French, and African history for several years at the Virginia Theological Seminary in Lynchburg, Virginia, where he became Dean in 1938; see also Okonkwo, "Orishatukeh Faduma," 31.

35. Okonkwo, "Orishatukeh Faduma," 31.

36. Okonkwo, "Orishatukeh Faduma," 31.

The Formative Years of the Collegiate School (1911–27)

Rev. Prof. Orishatukeh Faduma, BD, PhD (Yale)
Second Principal of the Collegiate School (1917–18)

With ethnocentric passion, the principal introduced the study of Mende and African folklore. By so doing, teaching in the vernacular became part of the curriculum at the UM Collegiate School.[37] The curriculum was further expanded to include Negro history and Arabic.[38] In addition to linguistic diversification and traditional courses for students in urban areas, farming or agriculture also became part of the curriculum. Further, Professor Faduma recommended that agriculture be taught in the rural areas. In blunt terms, he advocated education in race and pride:

> devotion to all that is excellent in race, glorifying in the noble achievement of its men and women, encouraging those in it who are striving and working towards a great idea.[39]

---

37. Okonkwo, "Orishatukeh Faduma," 27. It is most probable that the WAM Collegiate School was the first school in Freetown to introduce the teaching of a vernacular language into its curriculum (see the Bo School Prospectus of 1905).

38. *Sierra Leone Weekly News*, April 8, 1916, p. 6.

39. *Sierra Leone Weekly News*, April 8, 1916, p. 6.

The West African Methodist Collegiate School, 1911–2021

Consequently, Professor Faduma successfully integrated aspects of the African culture into the UM Collegiate School; a very revolutionary endeavor at the time.

The Afrocentric approach merely created an admixture of courses to embellish the composition of the traditional courses that were recognized and introduced by Principal Macauley—bookkeeping, arithmetic, Scripture, Latin, algebra, geometry, English language, music, and English literature.[40] Vigorous discipline, including appropriate dress codes, was maintained as a matter of continuity. Some students wore "Oxon and Tailcoat" to school. The attire of the students was a very captivating spectacle. An observer wrote,

> if you saw them some mornings going to class with their oxon and tailcoat and a big load of big books under their arms, you would think they were lawyers or some businessmen. They would pass round from Soldier Street gate through Price Street and entered [sic] into the Pademba Road building. You would think they were going to a wedding or to attend a Governor's party.[41]

The Faduma administration had a three-tiered court system, consisting of students, teachers, and the principal. The lower court was the court of original jurisdiction. Disputes that were not resolved in the lower court were then taken to the higher teachers' court. The principal constituted the appellate body. Implicitly, students were not expected to rush to the principal when they had disputes; they were expected to try and resolve disputes among themselves. The quasi-judicial structure (ad-hoc tribunal system) provided a mechanism through which discontents were arbitrated for the imposition of punishment on violators of the rules and regulations of the school.

Junior students were not encouraged to idly hobnob with senior students around the campus. Principal Faduma believed that the junior students must affiliate themselves with their cohorts. Students who violated such an expectation exposed themselves to corporal punishment.[42] The rationale is somewhat counterintuitive, but it was a motivational policy to encourage junior students to work harder to get to a privileged status in the school's hierarchy. With a very strong primary or private education, it was possible for a student to bypass the junior division of the educational

---

40. Interview (1984/5) with Mr. F. Thomas, a student of the school during the Faduma administration.

41. Pratt, *Autobiography*, 10.

42. Pratt, *Autobiography*, 10.

The Formative Years of the Collegiate School (1911–27)

hierarchy under Principal Faduma. The concession was ultimately dependent on the quality of knowledge about Latin, algebra, the definitions and propositions in Euclid and the Greek alphabets. A student was entitled to a spot in the Intermediate division of the senior level with the appropriate aptitude.[43] However, the students were rigorously challenged to excel.

By 1917, no one in the school was able to pass the Fourah Bay College Matriculation Examination or the Cambridge Senior Certificate Examination. It seemed as if the UM Collegiate School students did not understand the syllabus of the Fourah Bay College Matriculation Examination. One student observed:

> [I] passed in Arithmetic, Latin, Scripture, English Grammar, Literature and Composition, English History and Bookkeeping; but to get a Certificate, I should have passed in Geography or Euclid and Algebra which I did not take, because we did not understand the syllabus.[44]

However, in June 1918, the UMC members were very happy when for the first time in the history of the UM Collegiate School, one of its students, W. E. A. Pratt, passed the Fourah Bay College Matriculation Examination.

The Faduma administration was also interested in extracurricular activities. Collegiate students participated in sports and scouting activities; I subsequently became a Tenderfoot scout and a Patrol Leader in the 1980s. Under the Faduma administration, the school's football (soccer) team was able to defeat that of FBC on one occasion.[45] The cricket and athletics teams did not record notable successes. It was a common practice to have interschool and friendly competitions in soccer and cricket; usually, the venue for such competitions was the Tower Hill playing field or the Brookfields recreational arena.

Empire Day, May 24, was specifically set aside for recreational competitions. In commemoration of the day, all the schools in Freetown were given an opportunity to compete in athletics. The competitions were conducted with a great sense of individualism since the participants were not necessarily representing specific institutions.[46] The Brookfields recreational arena ("Recrea") was the most popular venue. Collegiate students participated vigorously and became famous for their performances in the sack

43. Pratt, *Autobiography*, 7.
44. Pratt, *Autobiography*, 10.
45. Pratt, *Autobiography*, 10.
46. Interviews (1984/5) with T. W. Clarkson and F. Thomas.

race, long-jump, and three-legged race. They were not very competitive in the pole vault or the egg-and-spoon race.[47]

Scouting provided an opportunity for students to make excursions to places of interests such as Hill Station, York, Tokeh, Number Two, Hamilton, and Sussex (villages on the outskirts of Freetown). The scouts were supervised by the Games Master (physical education teacher) and desiring teachers. Principal Faduma was able to make remarkable changes in the school within a period of two years.

He envisioned revolutionary changes not only for the UM Collegiate School but for the other secondary schools. One of his policies was not only to ensure the separation of church and state (something that he must have learned from America) but the duty of the government to support all schools. He presided over the Collegiate School at a time when the government was only providing capitation grants for all schools that were operated satisfactorily. Principal Faduma eventually resigned, because it became extremely difficult for the governors of the UM School to wholeheartedly embrace his visionary ambitions for the school.

Professor Faduma resigned the principalship of the school within the first two months of 1918 to work for the Department of Education of Sierra Leone as an Inspector of Schools. He taught at Model School for a brief period after his tenure at the UM Collegiate School. Indeed, Principal Faduma created an indelible impression on the minds of his students. Students provided a tribute to his service: "The good he has done, we do not think any other man will do for us."[48] By and large, the genre of education that he introduced to the school was characterized as *mente et manu* (education with the mind and hand).[49]

After the resignation of Principal Faduma, the UMC was revisited by the problem of finding a principal for the school. Since neither the BoGs nor the UMC Connexion in Freetown could find a replacement, the UMC branch in Freetown appointed the Rev. A. E. A. Greensmith (a European) to head the school. Apparently, the Rev. Greensmith was the Chairman of the District. The Rev. Greensmith served as principal till 1920, after which the Rev. J. B. Nicols was appointed the second time to act as principal of the

---

47. Interview (1984/5) with T. W. Clarkson.

48. See *The Sierra Leone Weekly News*, March 2, 1918, p. 12; see also Okonkwo, "Orishatukeh Faduma," 29.

49. See *Collegiate Diamond Jubilee Handbook 1911–1971*, 76.

The Formative Years of the Collegiate School (1911–27)

school. The Rev. J. B. Nicols served as acting principal till 1922 when the Rev. J. M. A. Johnson became principal.

Between 1919 and 1922, the school made progress with the help of the UMC officials in Freetown. The curriculum of the school was modified. Mende was eliminated and a course in "Procedures in Telegraphies" was introduced to the students. The new course in telegraphies was directed by the Rev. W. Micklethwaite. Students quickly nicknamed him the "*Rev. Eat- broke- plate*" because of the difficulties that were associated with the proper pronunciation of his name.[50] Traditional courses—like Latin, English literature and grammar, Scripture, English history, algebra, music, and arithmetic—were retained.

In 1922, W. E. A. Pratt was appointed to serve as Games and Scout Master of the school during the administration of the Rev. J. B. Nicols. It should be noteworthy that Mr. W. E. A. Pratt attended the Collegiate School in 1915. He had entered Fourah Bay College in 1919, but did part-time work at the Collegiate School. He taught students who were preparing for the Cambridge Junior Examination and subsequently became Junior Master. His areas of expertise were Latin, English literature and grammar, Scripture, and English history.[51] The scouts travelled to York (about twenty to twenty-five miles) on foot. They went through Hamilton to Tokeh, and would occasionally travel by boat from Tokeh, Number Two, and Sussex. The BoGs and the UMC in Freetown had difficulties finding a principal.

As a result of the inability to find a replacement, the BoGs and the UMC Connexion in Freetown decided to appoint the Rev. J. M. A. Johnson, MA, ACP, who had served as vice principal, to head the school in 1923. The principal, who was a staunch sportsman, elevated excitement to play cricket and lawn tennis. The school was comprehensively organized into three *Houses* for athletic competitions—Macauley, Faduma, and Greensmith.[52] The athletic *Houses* added another layer of competition that was distinct from the inter-school competitions. Drama and singing competitions became part of school life. Though the number of students increased since 1911, the number of students who were enrolled remained below 100 in 1925.[53]

---

50. Interview (1984/5) with Mr. J. R. Thorpe, senior member of the WAM church.

51. Pratt, *Autobiography*, 13.

52. Interview (1984/5) with Mr. F. Thomas. After the reopening of the School, Garber (of which I was a member) and Brown Nicols were added.

53. Pratt, *Autobiography*, 26.

Intermittent problems plagued the school by the turn of the 1920s and proposals were made to merge the UM Collegiate School with the Wesleyan Methodist Boys High School. Proposals were also made to merge the UMC with the Wesleyan Methodists. There was a consensus that religious synergies existed and that it was redundant to maintain the two schools as separate entities, given the population of students who desired secondary education in the Colony. Explicitly, the demand for education was too low to offset the cost of operating the schools.[54] Evidently, the financial situation of the UMC in Freetown was dire and precarious. Morale deteriorated in the school and it would seem that financial irregularities plagued the sustenance of the school.

The financial position of the school and the District was audited in 1926 by the Rev. E. Coker. It became apparent that while negotiations were ongoing for the unification or merger of the churches, the finances of the Collegiate School were in disarray.[55] The woeful and embarrassing situation forced the BoGs to demand the resignation of the principal to save the school and UMC Connexion in Freetown from scandal and litigation. Accordingly, the then General Superintendent, the Rev. J. B. Nicols approved the closure of the school in December 1927.

2.4 The Boarding Department (1911–27)

Boarding was an integral part of the operations of the school during the first period of the school's existence. Shortly after establishing the school, a boarding house was developed to house students from the Protectorate and beyond the confines of Sierra Leone. The building that faced Soldier Street was set aside for the boarders. By 1913, there were about twenty-three boarders but the numbers increased over time; for example, the number spiked after the strike in the CMS Grammar School.

The boarders had a regimen of their own. They woke up at 5:30 AM, showered, dressed, and attended classes in the morning. Breakfast was served before regular classes started at 7:30 AM, and lunch was served at noon. Dinner was served at about 7:30 PM to energize the students so that they can cope with their studies at night. It was the policy of the Boarding Department that every student should study till 9:30 PM, after

---

54. Interview (1984/5) with Mr. S. B. Moiba, an alumnus and acting principal of WAM Collegiate School (1975–1977).

55. Shodekeh-Johnson, "Growth and Development," 16.

which prayers were offered by the Boarding Home Master.[56] Teachers of the school performed the role of Boarding Home Master on a rotational basis. Messrs. T. J. V. Campbell and Everett Davies became two prominent Boarding Masters.

The lives of the boarders had some excitement. Fridays and Saturdays were regarded as "outing days" because boarders had an opportunity to go on excursions. By the 1920s, most of the teachers in Collegiate School had taken an interest in the boarding aspect of the school's life and they would take the boarders to their places of birth.[57] However, Messrs. E. Davies and W. E. A. Pratt normally took the boarders to Tower Hill, Model School, and Victoria Park (Sewa Grounds). The boarders also visited Regent, other mountainous villages, and coastal villages.

When visiting some of the mountainous villages like Regent, Gloucester, and Leicester, the boarders would board the "Mountain Train," moving from Hill Station to Water Street. The borders would then move to the Cotton Tree Station (the current location of the Sierra Leone Museum) and alight at the Hill Station stop before walking to their destination.[58] The boarders were usually under the supervision of Mr. O. P. A. Macauley when they went to Regent on "outing days."

When visiting coastal villages like Murray Town, Goderich, and Aberdeen, it was customary for the boarders to travel by boat from Murray Town to Aberdeen or the periphery of Aberdeen (the Cape). Mr. W. E. A. Pratt would take the borders to Hamilton, Sussex, Tokeh, and York villages. In describing life at the Boarding Department, Dr. W. E. A. Pratt wrote:

> Life in the Boarding Department was not too bad; in some sense it was good. But for the rustic or *'bush boy'* as the Freetown boys used to style us, the greatest problem was that of food, which was inadequate and badly prepared, especially at dinner time.[59]

Apparently, some of the boarders had a tough time in Freetown. The unpleasantness of boarding life weighed heavily on the poorer students. Wealthier students taunted the poorer students for not putting on attractive or expensive clothes. As the poorer students were being harassed, they would occasionally retort that the "cowl does not make the monk," *cucullus*

---

56. Moiba, "History of the Collegiate School," 16.
57. Interviews (1984/5) with Messrs. F. Thomas and T. W. Clarkson.
58. Interview (1984/5) with Mr. T. W. Clarkson.
59. Pratt, *Autobiography*, 10.

non facit monachum,[60] a Latin expression that was used to denote academic emptiness in fine or expensive clothing.

Apart from housing students beyond the confines of Freetown, boarding was a concept that also ensured the success of students in preparation for examinations. Invariably, the life of the boarders had a curious blend of academic rigor and fun. Boarders were taught the importance of agriculture and inspired to produce edible crops for their consumption.[61] Like every other aspect of the school's life, the life of the Boarding Department ended with the closure of the school in 1927.

2.5 The Interregnum and Mr. J. A. Garber (December 1927–February 1948)

The sadness of the closure of the school in 1927 was palpable. The Old Boys and the UMC agonized over the closure of a school that they had struggled to bring to fruition. Unsurprisingly, the Old Boys and the UMC relentlessly sought ways to reopen the school. It was customary for the church to have a Synod in the month of February known as the "Annual Assembly." The Synod made it possible for constituent parts of the church to appraise their work on an annual basis, iron out differences, make plans for forthcoming years, and formulate policies for the various districts.

Since the church was not too pleased about the closure of the school and the circumstances under which the operation of the school was suspended, the church reserved Collegiate School as an item on its agenda for deliberations. Some of the alumni and the UMC members in Freetown insisted that the school should be reopened. Prominent advocates for the re-opening included the Rev. J. B. Nicols, the Rev. I. S. T. Fewry (a foundation student), the Rev. E. A. E. Cole (a foundation student), Mr. J. A. Thomas, Mr. J. T. Nottidge, Mr. J. G. Hyde, Mr. R. I. A. Aubee, Mr. D. A. Williams, and Mr. J. A. Garber. The Old Boys Committee persistently held meetings after the closure of the school and became very vocal in putting forward proposals for the reopening of the school.

From the late 1920s to the 1930s, efforts to reopen the school were crippled by criticisms from different sources, including the then-Colonial Government. Officials of other secondary schools like the Albert Academy, the CMS Grammar School, and the Methodist Boys High School

---

60. Pratt, *Autobiography*, 10.
61. Interview (1984/5) with Mr. F. Thomas.

The Formative Years of the Collegiate School (1911–27)

condemned efforts to reopen the Collegiate School on the basis that the school was redundant.[62] There were obvious or inescapable underlying financial considerations, given the supply of prospective students in Freetown. Some of the former students of the UMC Collegiate School were already enrolled in some of the other schools in Freetown and former faculty members of the Collegiate School were already providing services to other academic institutions in Freetown. The competitive environment naturally fueled discontent and the resentment of reopening the Collegiate School.

The opposition to reopening the Collegiate School was further strengthened by a Colonial Government that had no interest in expanding Western-style secondary education in Freetown. The 1898 rebellion, Hut Tax War, had fomented animosity and generated displeasure for the proliferation of the Western form of education in Freetown. The reopening of the school reminded the Colonial Office of the toxic effect of education on the stability of colonial rule. The establishment of the Bo School in 1905 was a sordid reminder of an uncomfortable history. The Bo School was not to replicate the Western model. Part of the Bo School Prospectus reads:

> From the beginning of the Institution, the pupils will be taught that Labour is as necessary a part of Education as a knowledge of Reading, Writing, and Arithmetic. The main and primary object of the teaching will be to train the sons of chiefs in such a manner as to make them good and useful rulers of the country in the future . . .
>
> It is not the intention of the Government to employ any of the pupils after they shall have passed through the school . . .
>
> Each pupil [was] expected to bring 1 Country Gown, 1 White Gown, 3 Kerchiefs, 1 Cap, 1 Hammock (optional), [and] 1 Mat (country).[63]

However, in the second half of the 1940s, the UMC members and the alumni of the school decided to put more pressure on the Colonial Government. The Colonial Government, through the Director of Education, reluctantly gave permission to reopen the school on January 12, 1948. The permission to reopen the school was merely formal. Underlying logistics were not guaranteed and financing the reopening was unspectacularly precarious.

The UMC members and the Old Boys Committee faced incredible odds. There was no faculty and staff, no building (physical structure), and no determinative salary structure for the virtual school. At the time when

---

62. Interview (1984/5) with Mr. D. C. Thomas.
63. Fyfe, *Sierra Leone Inheritance*, 304–5.

the Colonial Government gave permission to reopen the Collegiate School, the school was not classified or listed as a "government-assisted school." Accordingly, the school was not qualified for financial assistance by the government though the proprietors (the alumni and UMC members in Freetown) of the school faced considerable financial hardship. In effect, the proprietors singularly had to carry the financial burden that was associated with the reopening of the school, including the salary for the principal.

Three names were considered for the principalship of the virtual school—the Rev. Dr. Fitz-John; Mr. D. A. Williams, BA, DipEd; and Mr. J. A. Garber, MA, LCP. Realizing that the salary will be fifty leones (Le 50.00) per month,[64] none but the altruistic Mr. J. A. Garber was willing to take up the challenge to run the virtual school. Mr. Garber, who was also a teacher at the CMS Grammar School some time ago, became the "sacrificial lamb." Teachers were offered twenty-five leones (Le 25.00) per month.[65] Evidently, the trifling salaries were not very attractive, and most teachers were not willing to work for a paltry amount of money that was far less than what could be obtained from the government-assisted schools.

Notwithstanding the meager salary, motivated and obliging teachers decided to work for the Collegiate School. Obliging teachers included: Mr. D. C. Thomas ("Master, Master"), London Matriculation; Mr. B. A. King (a student at Fourah Bay College at the time); Mr. D. E. Carney, BA, DPA; Mr. F. C. Dixon-Baker, London Matriculation; and Mr. C. A. Davies.[66] Securing a principal and some teachers made it rather feasible to proceed with the reopening of the school.

The absence of a viable structure for classes dashed the hopes of the Church and the alumni. Proactively aware of the problem, the principal-to-be, Mr. J. A. Garber, and some of the UMC Church members approached Mrs. Janet Butcher, the owner (landlady) of number 162 Circular Road, to see if the property could be leased. Mrs. Butcher was persuaded because the request was noble. Therefore, she consented to lease No. 162 Circular Road for the reopening of the Collegiate School.

The agreement with Mrs. Butcher, appertaining to the lease of the property, required the church to pay an annual rent of one hundred pounds (£100.00), approximately eight pounds (£8) a month. In 1960, the amount

---

64. Interview (1984/5) with Mr. S. T. Lewis-Nicol.
65. Interview (1984/5) with Mr. S. T. Lewis-Nicol.
66. Moiba, "History of the Collegiate School," 10.

was revised upwards to £250.00 per year.[67] With a principal, teachers, and structure, the reopening of the school was set for February 3, 1948. As arrangements were being made for the reopening of the school, the Education Department instructed the General Superintendent to postpone the reopening until the Divisional Engineer pronounced the building suitable for its intended purpose.

The BoGs awaited the Engineer's decision with a heavy heart. On the day of the inspection, the principal accosted the Engineer, Mr. Rice, but he surprisingly received a curt reply to his compliment. The reticent Engineer was unwilling to engage in any conversation with the principal. The Director of Education showed up a few minutes later after the arrival of the Engineer. The European Engineer started to make utterances like an oracle.

The Engineer condemned the wooden posts that supported the building and stated that they must give way to iron columns. Older men of the church had to go down to the Freetown Water Works Department to get iron columns and within an hour they returned, carrying columns on their shoulders. The building was retrofitted, subsequently reappraised by the Engineer, and pronounced suitable for use.

Members of the church who had sons and wards in secondary academic institutions elsewhere in Freetown decided to enroll their sons and wards in the newly re-established Collegiate School. The newly re-established school formally came into re-existence on February 3, 1948. However, unlike its former name, the UM Collegiate School, it was known as the West African Methodist (WAM) Collegiate School. The new name is attributable to reorganization of the UM and Methodist churches in 1935.

In 1932, there was another union of churches comprising the UMC and the Wesleyan and Presbyterian churches of England. The African Methodists lost some freedoms and privileges, which they had enjoyed as an independent body from 1844–1859, as a result of the union. Unlike the Western settlers, African Methodists did not have a say in the decisions of the church. Therefore, the African Methodists petitioned the church of England to redress their grievances.

A four-point memorandum was sent to the UM church in England. Instead of sending a direct response to the African Methodists, the UMCs sent a letter to the General Superintendent of the UMC, the Rev. A. E. Dymond, to be read in Synod. The essence of indirectly addressing the issue was to tie the hands of the African Methodists by the decisions that would

---

67. Interview (1984/5) with Mr. S. T. Lewis-Nicol.

have been made in Synod if the African Methodists had attended Synod.[68] Accordingly, the African Methodist Executive Committee decided not to attend the Synod. The African Methodists summoned a meeting on April 9, 1935 and adopted the name "West African Methodists,"[69] which was transferred over to the Collegiate School. The school was reopened with forty foundation students (see Table 2.2).

Table 2.2: Foundation Students in 1948

Name	Name	Name	Name
1. S. T. Lewis-Nicol	11. Charles Wilhelm	21. Siaka Kanu	31. Maurice Cassel
2. Salim Atib	12. Nicolas Paris	22. Gershon Coker	32. Ayodele Noah
3. Harleston Archibald	13. Moses Sandi	23. James Sango	33. Ronald Paris
4. George Cox	14. Onesimus Taylor	24. Gershoon Harding	34. Walter Nimmeh
5. Walter During	15. Oliver Refell	25. Bamidele Cole	35. Daniel Martin
6. John Dougan	16. Clarence Coker	26. Clarence Faukner	36. Cornelius Scott
7. Kobina Rennah	17. Basi Momoh	27. George Palmer	37. Arthur Lake
8. Ezekiah Taylor	18. James During	28. Albert Lewis	38. Oluwole Lemon
9. Alphonso Jones	19. Gibril Jalloh	29. Victor Thomas	39. William Macauley
10. Alphonso Clarke	20. Abdulai Fofanah	30. Olu Williams	40. Kambay Foster

2.6 The Principal, J. A. Garber, MA, LCP

Mr. Jonathan Abioseh Garber was born on a Sunday morning, July 23, 1905, at Waterloo village in Sierra Leone. He started to attend (infant) school

---

68. Shodekeh-Johnson, "Growth and Development," 18; also, the African Methodists perennially quarreled with the Wesleyans.
69. Shodekeh-Johnson, "Growth and Development," 18.

The Formative Years of the Collegiate School (1911–27)

at Blackhall Road,[70] after which he successfully proceeded to Standard School under Mr. Dixon. He took the Elementary Certificate Examination and, after attaining second place, he succeeded in obtaining a government scholarship. In 1919, he took the Intermediate Certificate Examination and completed his primary education at Waterloo.

After completing primary education, he proceeded to the CMS Grammar School in 1920 to obtain secondary education in Freetown. He matriculated in 1922 and attained the highest level of education at the school within three years. He earned a CMS scholarship in 1924 to enter Fourah Bay College, where he studied for a bachelor of arts degree and passed his first year examination in December 1924. He successfully passed his second and final year examinations in 1925 and 1927 respectively. Having successfully completed his undergraduate education in 1927, he pursued a master's degree in education at Durham University in 1934, which was conferred on him in 1935.

Principal Garber returned to the CMS Grammar School to teach English language and literature, Latin, Greek, Greek Testament, religious knowledge, and arithmetic—up to Cambridge Junior level—before he retired after twenty-five years at the CMS Grammar School.[71] He reentered academia as a result of the 1948 crisis at the Collegiate School. The resuscitation of the Collegiate School would have been most improbable without his altruism or selflessness. The home of the reestablished school, No. 162 Circular Road, was tentative and expedient. As the school expanded, it became necessary to provide a larger space for instruction and the administration of the affairs of the school. The next chapter is devoted to the operations of the school at Circular Road and the eventual movement to Wilkinson Road in Freetown.

---

70. *Collegiate Diamond Jubilee Handbook 1911–1971*, 22.
71. *Collegiate Diamond Jubilee Handbook 1911–1971*, 22.

3

The Collegiate School at Circular Road

AFTER THE SCHOOL WAS established at No. 162 Circular Road, it was not highly regarded and it lacked widespread recognition. Other secondary schools and the Colonial Government did not recognize the school. The school was not considered for the Common Entrance examination and it was not permitted to take part in inter-school's athletic competitions like singing, cricket, and soccer.[1] Additionally, the school was denied requests for government scholarships. Indeed, the teething period was one of abject neglect and isolation.

There were only two classes for the forty foundation students in 1948, consisting of preparatory Forms (Grades) 1 and 2. Since there were spatial problems, the school had to make use of the basement for devotion and the meetings of the Literary and Debating Society (L&DS). The L&DS meetings were presided over by fifth Form students (about fifteen by the early 1950s). It was mandatory for all students and teachers to attend the L&DS meetings,[2] which were usually conducted on the last two periods on Fridays. Guest speakers were occasionally invited to participate in debates. As time progressed, the basement was also utilized as a classroom for fifth Form students.

The uniform of the students of the Collegiate School was different from those of other schools. Students were required to wear black jackets

1. *Collegiate School's Diamond Jubilee Handbook 1911–1971*, 7.
2. Interview (1984/5) with Mr. S. T. Lewis-Nicol, foundation student (1948), Bursar and Confidential Secretary to Principal J. A. Garber in the 1950s, and Head Boy and Senior Prefect in 1952.

("coats"), white trousers, white shirts, black shoes, the school's tie (yellow alternating purple), a straw hat with a hat band made up of the school's colors, and the school's badge, which was worn by fifth Formers. The complete attire was subsequently reserved for ceremonial purposes because it was extravagantly formal for daily use and warm weather conditions. The decision to use the attire for formal occasions did not occur without rebellious fanfare. The Collegiate students were periodically taunted for their formal attire. As the students went to and from school, disrespectful onlookers would exclaim: "Old Coat!" "*Chinch* [bedbug] Coat!"[3] The uniform became an embarrassing symbol of elegance over which the students had no control. The school day started at 8 AM and ended at 2:30 PM. There was normally a break of about an hour, starting from 12:10 PM.

The proprietors of the school decided to run the school on a four-term basis. The first started from January and ended in March, the second started from March and ended in June, the third ran from July to September, and the fourth, from September to December.[4]

3.1 The School's Motto, Crest, and Song

A significant accomplishment of the school was the selection of a motto as part of its reestablishment. The school's motto, *"Plus Ultra"* (more beyond) is symbolic of the infinite dimension of learning. Specifically, no one should be presumptuous enough to think that he/she has acquired an infinite amount of knowledge (perfection). The motto draws inspiration from explorers who once felt that they had navigated the high seas to a point that it was humanly impossible to go any further.

In their practical knowledge of the world around them (*oikumene*), the Greek explorers were familiar with the Mediterranean and the Black Sea littorals. They also had considerable knowledge about the Caspian Sea, Persia, and the Western Coast of Europe.[5] In the 4th century BC, Greek navigators who reached the Pillars of Hercules—two rocks of Gibraltar flanking the entrance of the Mediterranean—inscribed the words, *"Ne Plus Ultra,"* on the rocks, meaning that it was not humanly possible to go beyond the Pillars of Hercules.[6] Pointedly, since the rocks were the highest

---

3. Interview (1984/5) with Mr. D. C. Thomas, foundation teacher in 1948.
4. Interview (1984/5) with Mr. D. C. Thomas, foundation teacher in 1948.
5. Penrose, *Travel and Discovery*, 2.
6. According to Greek mythology, it was believed that the mighty Hercules placed

The West African Methodist Collegiate School, 1911–2021

attainment ever reached by man, when early navigators reached the Pillars of Hercules they would go no further under the notion that they had accomplished all that was humanly possible on the high seas.

The Renaissance, rebirth of learning in Europe, altered the mythical misperception of the early Greek explorers. The renewed impetus to learn more about the world by exploration, revealed that there was more beyond the Pillars of Hercules and that the Pillars of Hercules could not possibly be a point of perfection; hence the phrase, *Plus Ultra*. Portuguese, English, French, and Spanish explorers took to the seas and conquered distant lands to expand trade and create markets. By reviving learning, ancient Greeks freed their minds and discovered that more could be uncovered (learnt) by undertaking risk and striving for excellence.

Charles V (February 24, 1500—September 21, 1558) adopted the motto *Plus Ultra* as the national motto of Spain, following the discovery of the New World by Christopher Columbus. Today, the motto is featured on both the flag and arms of Spain. The motto of the school is a tribute to extraordinary achievements that freed the imagination of mankind, the rebirth of learning. The Renaissance revealed "vistas of power and progress attainable by independent thought and resolute enquiry."[7]

Figure 3.1: The School's Crest and Motto

---

the two rocks in the Mediterranean and that no one could go beyond the rocks; see also *Collegiate Diamond Jubilee Handbook 1911–1971*, 11.

7. Penrose, *Travel and Discovery*, 2–3.

The Collegiate School at Circular Road

Beyond economic and religious motives, skepticism and curiosity conditioned the minds of humans to be adventurous; humans discovered that learning is an infinite process. A good number of voyages in the fifteenth and sixteenth centuries validated the preconditions for learning. Christopher Columbus, De Soto, and Prince Henry the Navigator—to name a few—debunked the myth of human perfection. The Greek mythology of perfection was no longer tenable after the voyages of discovery.

In addition to the school's motto, the crest was also developed as part of the accomplishments of the resuscitated school. The crest was designed by Sahr Foya, a member of the school, and it was officially commissioned in the early 1950s. Up to the early 1960s, only fifth Formers could put on the crest of the school. The decision to limit the use of the crest was based on aspirational considerations. It was believed that students who wanted to put on the crest will aspire to get to the fifth Form. The motto of the school was inscribed in the crest (see Figure 1). Further, the school's song was developed during the Garber administration. The title of the song, "Collegiate, Rah! Rah! Rah!," is a prominent and exhilarating refrain right through the song. The refrain was boisterously rendered with pride in the essence of the school. The school's song consists of five irregular but melodious verses. The first three verses are sung in virtually the same manner but the last two are unique (see the appendix to this chapter).

The words of the song convey the ideals of the school, prominent among which are "Truth, Justice, Honour, and Love for all." Principal Garber performed the brilliant and arduous task of putting the words of the school song together and turned the words over to the music teacher, Mr. C. A. Davies, to provide the music (score).[8] Invariably, the genius of the music has been credited to Mr. C. A. Davies. Consequently, the resuscitated school generated some amazing innovations with contemporaneous value—a motto, a crest, and a school song; notwithstanding, the school continued to face virtually insurmountable structural and financial challenges that were very dire by any reasonable standard of measurement. The principal entered into a phase of dire but surmountable struggles within the first two years of the existence of the resuscitated school.

---

8. Some organists of the alumni association in the United Kingdom—Christian Thomas, Ransford Grey, James Thorpe, and Emerson Jackson—have popularized the score; see Appendix 3A to this chapter.

3.2 Principal Garber and the Phase of Dire Struggle: February 1948 to the Second Half of the 1950s

The resuscitated school was bedeviled with problems from the outset. The school's building was expedient but obviously clumsy. It was meant to be a dwelling house and not the type of structure that would be expected for a normal school. As a result, it could not effectively serve the purpose of a school with an expanding student population. A lot of refurbishing and readjustment had to be undertaken as the school evolved.

Two rooms were eventually converted into a single classroom and blackboards were utilized as partition walls.[9] Unlike some other schools in Freetown, the WAM Collegiate School did not have a science laboratory. In a fortunate twist of events, the former owner of the Circular Road residence, Mr. Davies, was a baker. Mr. Davies constructed a bakery at the back of the house, which was effectively utilized as a laboratory until 1949. The principal encouraged the BoGs to take up tenancy of the bakery so that it could be converted into a science laboratory. The bakery was converted into a science laboratory in the first term of 1949 after accepting the proposal of the principal. There was an obvious shortage of science equipments and the school had to borrow equipments from other schools.

Inadequate finance was a constant source of inconvenience that tormented the administrators of the school. The financial situation prior to 1955 was very constraining because the onerous duty of administering and financing the operations of the school rested on the shoulders of the proprietors of the school. The absence of government subsidy made it extremely difficult to operate the school as a normal academic institution. The bulk of the revenue for operating the school came from the WAM church (Sierra Leone Connexion), and the paltry student tuition could not adequately finance the management of the school. Students were asked to pay two pounds, twelve shillings, and sixpence (£2.12s.6d) per term (semester).[10] The inadequacy of money (financial capital) resulted in an undesirable turnover of personnel.

The salary of the teachers at the WAM Collegiate School was not commensurate to that of the teachers who worked for government-assisted schools. The teachers of the Collegiate School had to precariously wait for their salaries; that is, it was not inevitable that the teachers will be paid or be

9. Interview (1984/5) with Mr. D. C. Thomas, DC.
10. Interview (1984/5) with Mr. S. T. Lewis-Nicol.

The Collegiate School at Circular Road

paid in a timely manner. Ironically, this unfortunate situation reoccurred in the 1980s when I was teaching history and government at the school. In the 1940s, the church had to secure funds from sources that were unreliable for the payment of salaries. The combination of precariousness and inadequacy of salary created push and pull conditions (push of personnel away from the Collegiate School and pull [attraction] toward the government-assisted schools). Further, Collegiate teachers had to use their meager salaries to subsidize the operation of the school by purchasing teaching supplies like chalk from local retailers, which compounded the doleful situation and misery of teaching.[11] Evidently, the proprietors of the school did not have the wherewithal to finance the operations of the school and government assistance was not forthcoming.

Invariably, inadequate (ponzi) finance reduced the motivation to teach at the Collegiate School, and the demoralized Collegiate teachers could not sustain the excitement and commitment that they had summoned in 1948 to facilitate the successful resuscitation of the school. Despondent Collegiate School teachers sought attractive alternatives in government-assisted schools and walks of life with competing salaries. The financial reality naturally caused the turnover of staff (instability) at the Collegiate School in the 1940s. Table 3 identifies the strength of the staff between 1948 and 1952.

Between 1948 and 1952, some of the members listed in Table 3.1 started to look for better opportunities; for example, Mr. D. E. Carney, who was responsible for mathematics in the second Form, left the school at the end of the first term in 1948 for the post of Statistician with the Nigerian Government. Mr. C. A. O. Davies resigned his appointment as a full-time teacher for a lucrative appointment in Liberia. In June 1952, Mr. J. E. Aubee left for the United Kingdom; Mr. D. E. Chaytor, a Science Master, left for the Prince of Wales; Mr. E. Tugbah Thompson subsequently resigned; and Mr. Griffin, who was teaching mathematics and science, was asked to resign because of negligent work.[12] The principal had to search for new teachers.

The principal and school administrators were able to recruit qualified replacements under propitious or fortunate circumstances. New recruits included: Mr. George Cox, BA, Dunelm; Mr. S. H. Kanu; Mr. S.T. Lewis-Nicol (a strict disciplinarian); Mr. Dan Davies; Mr. Lengar

---

11. Interview (1984/5) with Mr. D. C. Thomas (foundation teacher, 1948).
12. Moiba, "History of the Collegiate School," 16–22.

Koroma; Mr. Vidal Godwin; Mr. A. O. Smith (Albaya); Mr. N. A. Hayes, BSc; Mrs. Caroline Roy-Macauley; Miss Vastia Pratt; Mr. J. N. Edwin; and Mr. L. C. Green, BA, DipEd.[13]

In addition to staffing problems, the structural or spatial problem continuously festered in the 1950s. The number of students increased on an annual basis without any corresponding increase in the spatial structures. When school started on January 24, 1949, thirty students were admitted. At the start of that year, the number of students on roll increased to seventy-five, with a greater number in the Junior Cambridge Form. By the end of the year, the number of students on roll was about 120. When the school reopened on January 22, 1951, the number increased to 140. In a week prior to the reopening of the school from vacation (in 1952), fifty new students were admitted. In sum, by the end of the year, there were about 215 students on roll for a building that had housed forty students in 1948. By the end of 1952, Form 1 consisted of three streams with 120 students. Form 2 consisted of forty-five students, one stream of Form 3 had twenty-eight students, and one stream of Forms 4 and 5 had a cumulative enrollment of twenty-two students.

13. Moiba, "History of the Collegiate School," 16–22.

The Collegiate School at Circular Road

Table 3.1: Staff of the WAM Collegiate School (1948–52*)

Name (1948–49)	Name (1950–52)
Mr. J. A. Garber, MA, LCP (Principal, 1948)	Mr. E. Tugbah Thompson, LMC (1950)
Mr. D. E. Carney, BA, DPA (1948)	Mr. D. E. Chaytor (1952)
Mr. B. A. King, TC, LMC (1948)	Mr. V. J. Hastings-Spaine
Mr. C. A. O. Davies (1948)	Mr. W. O. Pratt
Mr. F. C. Dixon-Baker, LMC (1948)	Mr. J. E. Aubee
Mr. D. C. Thomas (1948)	
Mr. A. E. Griffin (1949)	
Mr. A. O. Oduyumgbo (1949)	

*Mr. E. Tugbah Thompson joined the staff on January 23, 1950 and Mr. V. J. Hastings-Spaine was a student at Fourah Bay College.[14]

On January 10, 1955, the school started classes with about 329 students on roll. There were three streams of Form 1, consisting of 118 students, three streams of Form 2, consisting of ninety-three students, one stream of Form 4, comprising of seventeen students, and a stream of Form 5 with seventeen students.[15] Unsurprisingly, there were about 338 students on roll by December 1957 and it became refractory to manage the student population under the structural constraints that existed; there was an evident problem of overcrowding.

By 1954, the basement of No. 162 Circular Road was congested. When the Director of Education made a visit to the school that year, he condemned a portion of the basement and declared it unsuitable for the congregation of classes. Divisions that were made by screens were considered to be unseemly and improper for classes. Spatial and financial difficulties compelled the BoGs to apply to the Education Department for inclusion in the list of government-assisted schools. After a full dress inspection on September 11

14. Moiba, "History of the Collegiate School," 16–22.
15. Moiba, "History of the Collegiate School," 16–22.

and 12, 1952, the Director of Education promised to consider the request. In 1955, the Minister of Education, Hon. A. M. Margai, conceded that the school must be considered for full grant after he inspected the school at Circular Road. The reasonable consideration of the Minister made it possible for the Collegiate School to be considered for full grant in 1955.[16] Notwithstanding the conclusion, problematic congestion continued.

In 1956, the situation in the basement of No.162 Circular Road became uncontrollable and the principal was forced to look for pressure release valves or outlets. It became apparent that only spatial expansion could redress the impractical situation. The principal then proceeded to request the lease of an additional structure—a neighboring basement—belonging to Mr. O. P. A Macauley. The principal negotiated with Mr. Macauley for the use of his basement at No. 157 Circular Road and Mr. Macauley agreed to lease the adjoining basement for three pounds (£3) per month.[17]

The acquisition of the basement at No. 157 Circular Road was a welcomed relief. The newly acquired structure purposefully served the fifth Formers. The structure was used as a classroom for the fifth Formers from 1956 to 1960 but the proprietors of the school considered the structural relief to be inadequate, temporary, and unsustainable. The principal made a request for the government to erect three classrooms on a military strip of land at the back of the school. One of the classrooms was expected to serve as a makeshift science laboratory. The government declined to engage in the expansion.

Between 1956 and 1957, the principal spent three months in the United Kingdom; Mr. B. A. King acted as principal. The Head of the Institute of Education at the University of London, Dr. Jeffrey, made it possible for Principal Garber to visit six schools in London—two modern secondary schools, two comprehensive schools, one grammar school, and one public school.[18] Principal Garber expanded his knowledge about the operations of secondary schools and exploited the opportunity to purchase equipments for the Collegiate School. In the interim, the student population continued to increase.

In the 1950s, the proprietors of the Collegiate School were compelled to construct another building at the back of No. 162 Circular Road as the student enrollment in the Collegiate School increased. The building

16. Interview (1984/5) with Mr. S. T. Lewis-Nicol.
17. Interview (1984/5) with Mr. S. T. Lewis-Nicol.
18. Moiba, "History of the Collegiate School," 32.

became known as the "four-classroom-prefab building." The construction of the prefab building was the result of proactive planning that had been in the works for about two to three years; progress had been retarded because of a delay in delivering building materials. Arcon Roof building materials arrived in October 1956. The Blastons Building Construction Company was granted the contract to construct the building after the receipt of the building materials and consultations with contractors.[19]

Construction started in late November 1956 and by the end of January 1957 the building was available to be occupied. The classrooms were dedicated on Wednesday January 30, 1957 and originally reserved for morning devotion and meetings of the L&DS.[20] Part of the school occupied the building until the school moved to Wilkinson Road in 1961. The building was later leased by the Freetown City Council for use by one of its primary schools, the Fort Street Municipal School. Significantly, the spatial and financial problems of the school did not adversely affect the academic performance of the Collegiate students.

The school had its first outstanding academic success in 1949 when two students out of four successfully passed the Junior Cambridge Examinations (with one distinction in history). The following year, two students, Shaka H. Kanu and George Cox, also passed the same exam. The result was also replicated in 1951 when Harleston Archibald and Victor Thomas passed the exam. In 1955, four students attempted the School Certificate, General Certificate Examinations (GCE), and all were successful, including J. S. Momoh (who eventually became Major General of the Sierra Leone Military Forces and President of Sierra Leone).[21]

Frequent visits by inspectors of schools and observers of the West African Examination Council (WAEC) incentivized the proprietors of the school to constantly make readjustments for improved and acceptable conditions. In the mid 1950s, a report made by WAEC admonished the school to take science subjects (courses) more seriously. In response, the school increased its interest in science and spent four hundred pounds (£400.0) on chemical equipments in 1957. The government also assisted in elevating the profile of science by providing a grant of two hundred and fifty pounds (£250.00).[22] The financial support made it possible for the school to offer

19. Moiba, "History of the Collegiate School," 35.
20. Interview (1984/5) with Mr. S. T. Lewis-Nicol.
21. Interview (1984/5) with Mr. S. T. Lewis-Nicol.
22. Moiba, "History of the Collegiate School," 33.

physics up to Form 3 by the second half of the 1950s. Since the school was struggling to get an appropriate science laboratory, the school deposited two hundred pounds (£200.00) with a firm in England to commence work on a physics laboratory. Apart from scientific equipments, the scientific library was under-resourced.

In the 1940s and 1950s, the school ordered scientific books and school equipments from Bowes and Bowes in England and Phillips and Tacey respectively. The results of the purchases did not make the school a well-resourced repository of scientific resources. The deficiency of scientific resources invigorated commitment and resolve to enhance the holdings of the scientific library. Three hundred pounds (£300.00) were allocated by the school for the purchase of scientific equipments and books. The larger budgetary allocation for books made it possible to purchase large reference books and teaching aids for the faculty members. Teaching aids in the form of pamphlets, charts, periodicals, and magazines added value to the scientific collection of the school's library. A considerable amount of the changes that took place in the second half of the 1950s ushered in the dawn of an era of reconstruction.

3.3 The Era of Reconstruction and the School at Wilkinson Road

In the aftermath of the recognition for full grant in 1955, the financial situation of the school auspiciously changed for the better. As the government subsidized the financial expenditures of the school, the government was also drawn into the structural or spatial plans for the expansion of the school and the concomitant expenditures that were associated with such plans. The proprietors of the school were no longer willing to make incremental and ad hoc plans for the expansion of the school in constrained spaces. Accordingly, they preferred a more lasting, permanent, and sustainable structure that was capable of absorbing an expanding student population. The proprietors of the school started to search for a spot that was sufficient to construct a structure that was capable of containing a minimum of 500 students. The principal considered proximity and space at the back of No. 162 Circular Road, which would have made it easier to rapidly transport the assets (property and equipments) of the school. The Minister

The Collegiate School at Circular Road

of Housing and Country Planning, Hon. Cyril Rogers-Wright, opposed the idea because the land belonged to the Crown.[23]

Consequently, alternative efforts were made to purchase land behind Albert Academy in Freetown. Once again, the government opposed the proposition because of the propensity to concentrate schools in one geographic area.[24] A novel opportunity arose immediately after a series of setbacks. Some of the WAM church members in Freetown—Mr. Ajaye Thomas, Mr. J. N. K. Brown, and Mr. J. Zizer—were able to persuade the owner of a vast area of land at Wilkinson Road, Mr. Zuzay, to sell the land to the proprietors of the school.[25] The proprietors were very willing to almost exhaust their finances to acquire what was a luxurious space of land that was far away from the center of Freetown. On the occasion of the opening of the school at Wilkinson road, the principal observed,

> fifty years ago when the first Collegiate School was opened, no one would have thought of building a school on this plot. It was the time when there was no Wilkinson Road and only a footpath lay between Congo Town and Lumley. This land was then wooded and was the favourite resort for hunters. In the Second World War the land was used as one of the Military Camps in Sierra Leone and was the scene of many military parades. After the military left it, its tall grass provided graze for cattle. Now the use of the land has improved. We feed our boys with food for mind and body. We drill them to become citizens and we hunt and sort the various types of intelligence for specific training.[26]

The architect's report pays tribute to an enviable location:

> The view of the land is superb as seen from site photographs, there being an unobstructed view of the Aberdeen Creek and Aberdeen point with the open sea behind.... The buildings stand having the hills in front and the sea behind them.[27]

The government was notified about the purchase of the land at Wilkinson Road, and at the beginning of February 1956, the Town Planning

---

23. Interviews (1984/5) with Messrs. D.C. Thomas, and S.T. Lewis-Nicol.
24. Interviews (1984/5) with Messrs. D.C. Thomas, and S.T. Lewis-Nicol.
25. Interview (1984/5) with Mr. F. Thomas.
26. Principal Garber's speech on the occasion of the official opening of the WAM Collegiate School at Wilkinson Road, 1961, (see Appendix 3B).
27. Principal Garber's speech on the occasion of the official opening of the WAM Collegiate School at Wilkinson Road, 1961, (see Appendix 3B).

Officer and the Medical Officer of Health granted the principal permission to commence the construction of the new school buildings. The then-Minister of Education, Hon. A. M. Margai, is generally considered to be the "benefactor of the Collegiate School."[28]

The Minister saw the reconstruction of the school as an African venture that should be encouraged. Through his individual efforts, the Colonial Development and Welfare Funds provided seventy-seven thousand pounds (£77,000.0) for the erection of two large blocks—a four-storied science block and a three-storied classroom block.[29] The government gave sixty thousand pounds (£60,000.0) as financial contribution to the construction of the new school.[30]

After securing a reasonable amount of money, the principal notified the Education Department that the school was about to start the construction of a new structure under a private contractor, Mr. S. E. Luke. The Education Department raised a number of objections. Public tenders for the construction were not issued and the qualification of the contractor was called into question. The government rejected the idea of not issuing a public tender for a building project that obtained a grant from the Colonial Development and Welfare Fund.[31] Remarkably, the proprietors of the school had made an agreement with a contractor, which exposed the proprietors to legal liability for a breach of contract.

The Education Department issued directives that construction must be halted just before Mr. Luke started work. Mr. Luke had planned to erect a big building that would contain the classrooms and the laboratory, and he had expended labor to draw up plans for the construction of the building. The government ultimately decided to award the contract through a Tender Board, which issued a contract for the construction of buildings to the Public Works Department (PWD) in 1958.

According to the new tender, cost for the laboratory and classroom buildings was estimated to be sixty-five thousand pounds (£65,000.0).[32] No completion date was provided by the PWD but it was assumed that

28. Alison-Konteh, "Changing Phase," 5.

29. Interview (1984/5) with Mr. S. T. Lewis-Nicol.

30. "The Collegiate School Scheme D. 1340 ref. No.IN/26/1, April 1, 1960," The WAM Collegiate School File, Ministry of Education, Freetown.

31. Interviews (1984/5) with Messrs. S. T. Lewis-Nicol and D. C. Thomas.

32. "The Collegiate School Scheme D. 1340 ref. No.IN/26/1, April 1, 1960," The WAM Collegiate School File, Ministry of Education, Freetown.

construction would have been completed between fifty-two and seventy-two weeks; the proposed time span was an extrapolation from the offers of competing contractors.[33] In keeping with the budgetary estimate of the PWD, the proprietors of the school estimated that seventy-seven thousand pounds (£77,000.0) would give them administrative blocks, science laboratories, classrooms, an assembly hall, wood workshop, and quarters for the principal and staff.[34]

The hopes of the proprietors were dashed when it became apparent that the PWD had made some financial miscalculations. Shortly after commencing construction, PWD officials revised the original estimate. In a letter issued by the Director of Education, Mr. W. G. Jones, dated April 1, 1960, the amount was revised upwards to seventy-two thousand pounds (£72,000.0).[35] The earlier estimate had omissions—fencing (£1,500.0), layout of groundwater and surface water drainage (£850.0), electricity (£2,000.0), and water (£950.0).[36]

The Director's clarification and progress report indicated that the sixty-five thousand pounds (£65,000.0), voted for the buildings, could only provide administrative blocks, science laboratories, and classrooms. It was projected that the discrepancy between the estimate of the proprietors (£77,000.0) and the original estimate of the PWD (£65,000.0), twelve thousand pounds (£12,000.0), could have been used to construct an assembly hall. As efforts progressed to construct the buildings, the original contractor, Mr. S. E. Luke, sued the BoGs for a breach of contract. The BoGs circumstantially compensated Mr. Luke for work that had been previously undertaken and construction progressed.[37]

By February of 1960, 80 percent of the science block was completed. Plumbing for gas and water supplies had been completed and electrical wiring was about 75 percent complete. Shelving in the library and bookstore, fixing of glass louvre blades to louvred windows, final screeding to floors, and the construction of timber-framed dais to the laboratories were

---

33. "The Collegiate School Scheme D. 17001(D)/11/53, September 30, 1960," The WAM Collegiate School File, Ministry of Education, Freetown.

34. "The Collegiate School Scheme D. 17001(D)/11/53, September 30, 1960," The WAM Collegiate School File, Ministry of Education, Freetown.

35. "The Collegiate School Scheme D. 1340 ref. No.IN/26/1, April 1, 1960," The WAM Collegiate School File, Ministry of Education, Freetown.

36. "The Collegiate School Scheme D. 17001(D)/11/53, September 30, 1960," The WAM Collegiate School File, Ministry of Education, Freetown.

37. Interview (1984/5) with Mr. D. C. Thomas.

incomplete. Similarly, sanitary fittings and internal and external decorations were incomplete.[38]

The amount of work that was incomplete made it impossible to complete construction of the buildings within the maximum anticipated period of seventy-two weeks. The arrival of laboratory furniture and electrical fittings was late. In a letter to the proprietors on June 16, 1960, the Acting Director of Public Works, Mr. G. Skely, stated that work would not be completed until December 1960. The estimated completion date was fifteen weeks in excess of earlier projection.

Work was actually completed in February 1961 and two buildings were functional—the classroom structure and science laboratory. Seventy-two thousand pounds (£72,000.0) provided by the governments of the United Kingdom and Sierra Leone were used to construct the science and classroom blocks. The ground floor consisted of four classrooms—the staff room, the principal's office, and two toilets at the ends of the floor. The first and second floors had six classrooms with two toilets at both ends. The basement of the laboratory block housed the school's library. The first, second, and third floors of the laboratory block housed the physics, biology, and chemistry laboratories respectively. All the laboratories had junior and senior sections.

The buildings were opened on February 15, 1961, during the principalship of Mr. J. A. Garber, who worked extraordinarily hard to resuscitate and put the Collegiate School on a viable or sounder footing. The opening ceremony was conducted on the forecourt of the school under the chairmanship of the Hon. A. M. Margai. The Governor of Sierra Leone, Sir Maurice Dorman, KCMG (who took the leading role in the official opening of the school); Lady Dorman, the Aide-de-Camp to the Governor; Mr. H. M. Lynch-Shylon; the Rev. I. S. T. Fewry (the General Superintendent of the WAM church and Chairman of the BoGs); the Rev. D. M. Shears; Mr. J. T. Nottidge, the Mayor of Freetown; and Alderman A. F. Rahman, OBE, JP, were among the distinguished guests. An assembly of well over two thousand people, representing prominent businesses and consisting of citizens, took part in the celebration.[39]

The Rev. I. S. T. Fewry conducted prayers and the principal made a speech to commemorate the occasion (see Appendix 3B). The principal

---

38. M. P. New (D)42, Public Works Department, Newsletter, February, 1960, The WAM Collegiate School File, Ministry of Education, Freetown, 9.

39. Interview (1984/5) with Mr. S. T. Lewis-Nicol.

recognized the attendance of the governor and commended him for accepting an invitation by the WAM church to a celebratory occasion that was "exclusively theirs." Principal Garber described the site on which the buildings were constructed. The site was a treasure for hunters, soldiers, and cattle rearers. The use of the land was improved for feeding the minds and bodies of students. Metaphorically, the WAM Collegiate students were being drilled to become good citizens on a land that had been used by hunters and soldiers during and after the Second World War. Further, the speech alluded to the founding of the school in 1911 and, as a matter of evolutionary reminiscence, recalled the formidable challenges that became existential threats to the existence of the school.

Sir Maurice Dorman, KCMG (1957)
Governor of Sierra Leone (1956–61)
Governor-General of Sierra Leone (1961–62)

The Governor, Sir Maurice Dorman, declared the buildings opened after the principal delivered his commemorative speech. A tour of the buildings followed the opening formalities. The governor espoused great interest in science and raised a number of questions that were answered by the physics teacher, Dr. Willie Young.[40] The ceremony ended seventeen years of turbulence and spatial agony. A European visitor, Mr. Borys, told

---

40. Interview (1984/5) with Mr. S. T. Lewis-Nicol.

the Chairman of the Central Tender Board, Mr. A. Macleod-Smith, that he considered the finish on the WAM Collegiate School building to be "superior to any other school building designed by this firm [sic]."[41]

Rev. I. S. T. Fewry, OBE
Alumnus and General Superintendent of the WAM Church

Several donations were made to the school after the celebration. Shell Company donated eight hundred pounds (£800.0) to equip the chemistry laboratory; the Mining Association donated four-hundred pounds (£400.0) to equip the physics laboratory; and two thousand dollars ($2000.0) came from the United States for the laboratories. A set of Encyclopedia Britannica was donated by the United States to be used in the library. Some alumni of the school also made significant contributions; for example, Mr. Augustine Stevens sent the human skull in plastic form for the biology laboratory while he was studying in the United States. Mr. George Cox

---

41. C.T.B/16, March 7, 1960, The WAM Collegiate School File, Ministry of Education, Freetown.

The Collegiate School at Circular Road

sent six volumes of world history while he was studying at New Brunswick University in Canada.[42]

The movement of the school to Wilkinson Road was not immediate. The school continued to operate at Circular Road for quite some time after the opening ceremony. However, by the second half of 1961, some students who were itching to move to Wilkinson Road started to become restless. The principal and the proprietors decided that the school should move to Wilkinson Road by the second half of 1961. The decision was made after the school was furnished with brand new furniture from Britain.

The school eventually started at Wilkinson Road with about 500 students.[43] The opening of the school also coincided with a Collegiate uniform/dress-reform movement. It must be recalled that the Collegiate students had been taunted for their elegant uniform when they were at Circular Road. Tired of putting on the formal attire of jackets, ties, and straw hats, the students revolted and some of them hung their jackets on the fence of the school. As a result of the dress reform agitation, the school decided to adopt a regular day uniform consisting of grey shorts and white short-sleeved shirts, while retiring the formal attire for ceremonial purposes only. Fifth Formers were permitted to wear pants (longer versions of shorts) and long-sleeved shirts.

Without sufficient money to construct an assembly hall—thanks to the miscalculation of cost by the PWD—the passageway connecting the laboratories and the classrooms was utilized for morning assembly (morning religious services).[44] Obviously, the passageway was not suitable for morning devotion and could not be considered to be a chapel. Therefore, its use was temporary and expedient. In 1962, plans were made to construct an assembly hall.

The foundation stone of the assembly hall was laid on February 14, 1962. The ground on which the assembly hall was to be constructed was ceremonially consecrated by the then-General Superintendent of the WAM church, the Rev. I. S. T. Fewry, who performed what was regarded as the "turning of the sod."[45] The Minister of Education, Mr. H. E .B. John, and the General Superintendent of the Methodist Church in Sierra Leone, the

---

42. Interview (1984/5) with Mr. S. T. Lewis-Nicol.
43. Interview (1984/5) with Mr. S. T. Lewis-Nicol.
44. L. J. Y. Coker, alumnus and Bursar at the School (interview, 1984/5).
45. Sierra Leone Broadcasting Service, News, February 14, 1962, The WAM Collegiate School File, Ministry of Information, Freetown.

Rev. W. E. A. Pratt, were among hundreds of WAM church members and children who witnessed the ceremony. The officiating priests included: the Reverends C. H. Q. Russel, E. A. E. Cole, D. H. Shears, and J. A. D. Davies.[46]

The Assembly Hall was completed in January 1965 with a capacity to hold about 600 students plus the members of staff and the school attained spatial convenience in 1965. Within a few years after the establishment of the school at Wilkinson Road, the school provided facilities for physics, biology, and chemistry, and space for history, geography, Bible knowledge, Latin, English language, and English literature, *inter alia*. Below the fifth Form, all courses were considered to be core courses. The reconstruction of the WAM Collegiate School was a phenomenal occurrence. Alison-Konteh writes:

> the Collegiate School which could not afford the luxury of teaching Science subjects now offers all branches of Science. . . . From his large reservoir of experience and wisdom, Principal Garber did not and has not accepted the practice of making public examination an end in a pupil's career to warrant making his school a school certificate or G.C.E. merchant. Instead, he has maintained his policy of giving his pupils a general course of studies, allowing selection of Subjects or Specialization after crossing the fourth form of the school. This policy has not jeopardized the progress of the school in public examinations as the school records show a fifty percent pass in the 1962/63 School Certificate Examination with one first division and four second division passes . . . the 1963/4 results showed greater success with 80% passes.[47]

The revitalized government-assisted school was able to recruit and retain qualified teachers (see Table 3.2)[48]

---

46. Sierra Leone Broadcasting Service, News, February 14, 1962, The WAM Collegiate School File, Ministry of Information, Freetown.

47. Alison-Konteh, "Sir Albert Presides," 4.

48. Interview (1984/5) with Mr. S. T. Lewis-Nicol.

The Collegiate School at Circular Road

Table 3.2: Staff of the WAM Collegiate School in 1964*

Name	Name
Mr. J. A. Garber, MA, LCP (Principal, 1948)	Miss Alice Kamara, BA, DipEd.
Mr. B. A. King, BA (1948)	Mr. S. T. Lewis Nicol (1952/3)
Mr. D. C. Thomas, BA, Inter. (1948)	Mr. A. O. Beckley, BSc, DipEd.
Mr. V. J. Hastings-Spaine BA, DipEd (1950/2)	Mr. George Cox, BA (1952/3)
Mr. W. A. Koyenikan, Certificate in Education	Mrs. A. Fitz-John, Certificate in Education

*Starting career with the school in parenthesis

The school held its first prize-giving ceremony at Wilkinson Road on January 13, 1965, which was presided over by Sir Albert Margai. The principal considered Sir Albert Margai to be a "benefactor of the Collegiate School" and a play, entitled "Web of Circumstances" was dramatized by some students.[49]

In his address, the Chairman appealed to all Sierra Leoneans to be generous in their attitudes to development projects, especially education. "The Collegiate School of today and progress it has made," he asserted, is a "proof of Principal Garber's indomitable courage, determination, hard work, and perseverance."[50] In a short address to the students, the Guest Speaker, Professor Eldred Jones (later principal of Fourah Bay College, University of Sierra Leone), informed the students that education transcends "book learning" to include discipline, strength, and willpower to exercise self-control in times of difficulties. The English Professor recalled the play, *Web of Circumstances*, to show why restraint should be meaningful in the daily lives of students.[51] Pointedly, wrong behavior is not a way to project strength for temporary glory. It is better to go into the wilderness alone than err with the crowd (herd mentality).

49. Alison-Konteh, "Sir Albert Presides," 5.
50. Alison-Konteh, "Sir Albert Presides," 5.
51. A boy with a violent temper refrained from returning a blow even under extreme provocation in the play.

Part of the prize-giving ceremony included the unveiling of two photographs of the late Archdeacon C. A. E. Macauley and the late Rev. J. Brown Nicols (former principals of the school). The unveiling ceremony, which took place in the school's assembly hall, was performed by Mrs. Agnes Smythe-Macauley, widow of Archdeacon Macauley, and Miss Reffel, a niece of the late Rev. J. B. Nicols. Mr. V. Hastings-Spaine gave the vote of thanks and prizes were distributed by Mrs. R. I. A. Aubee. A number of luminaries graced the occasion—Mr. A. H. Kandeh (Parliamentary Secretary to the Prime Minister), Mr. Gershon Collier (a United Nations representative), the Force Commander and his wife, Mrs. Lansana, Justice R. B. Marke, Mr. W. F. Conton (the Chief Education Officer), and Rev. Dr. William Fitz-John.[52]

J. A. Garber, Esq., MA (Dunelm), LCP
Principal of the Collegiate School (1948–65)

After shepherding the institution for over seventeen years, the health of Principal Garber deteriorated and he had to hand over the reins of authority to someone else. In December 1965, Principal Garber retired and handed over the principalship to Mr. Hastings-Spaine for the next four years. Alison-Konteh provided a fitting tribute to the principal:

> Despite the buffets of the trying years of the school's infancy, Principal Garber and the mission doggedly plodded on with tenacity of

---

52. Alison-Konteh, "Sir Albert Presides," 5.

purpose to steer this educational boat from the tempestuous seas to a shore far beyond the horizons of the short-sighted opponents.[53]

Indeed, the Garber-era was a period of unimaginable challenges that redefined the history and resilience of the school. From the verge of extinction, Principal Garber resuscitated the Collegiate School and unrelentingly ensured that the school was left on a sound and sustainable foundation. The "Second Collegiate School," as the school was occasionally regarded, handed down unique features of modernization and charted a path that will last for several generations to come. It is highly probable that there would have been no "Second Collegiate School" without Principal J. A. Garber.

---

53. Alison-Konteh, "Sir Albert Presides," 4.

4

The Administration of Mr. Hastings-Spaine (1966–71)

LIKE HIS PREDECESSORS, MR. Hastings-Spaine was not an alumnus of the school. He attended the CMS Grammar School. You may recall that he had been a part-time teacher at the Collegiate School after the school was resuscitated in 1948. In 1958, he graduated with a bachelor's degree from Fourah Bay College and in 1962 he obtained a Diploma in Education. He went to London on two occasions (1963/4) to further his education and obtained a Diploma in Educational Administration from Reading. He became principal of the Collegiate School in 1966.

4.1 The Administration

The start of the Hastings-Spaine administration was rather turbulent, because some teachers were not too receptive of his appointment. They considered him to be a junior teacher before his appointment. At the time of his appointment, Messrs. B. A. King and W. O. Pratt were considered to be senior faculty members; for example, Mr. King taught Mr. Hastings-Spaine at the CMS Grammar School.[1] Quite apart from teaching Mr. Hastings-Spaine, Mr. King had acted as principal of the school when Mr. Garber was unavailable. Many teachers were sympathetic with the situation of Mr. B. A. King.

One school of thought maintained that there were ill feelings between Principal Garber and Mr. King by the end of Mr. Garber's tenure. As a result,

---

1. Interview (1984/5) with Mr. B. A. King.

The Administration of Mr. Hastings-Spaine (1966-71)

Principal Garber groomed Mr. Hastings-Spaine for the position. Some faculty members joined the staff during this period—Mr. Superneker, BSc, BT, MEd (who eventually taught me mathematics); Mr. A. Beckley, BSc, DipEd; Mr. Victor Cozier (GCE A Level); and Mr. S. B. Moiba, BA, DipEd.[2]

Mr. Hastings-Spaine brought some innovations to the school and preserved the older curriculum. He provided more chairs for students, made arrangements for transportation of students to school, and resurfaced the field of the school for student recreation.[3] Mr. G. B. Ollivant was given the contract for the supply of new chairs. Inadequate chairs had been part of the internal problems in the school. The General Engineering and Construction Company was granted a contract for resurfacing and reconditioning of the school's field.

A year after assuming office, the principal launched one of the athletic Houses, Garber, for athletic competition. It was a fitting tribute to the indefatigable work of Principal Garber.[4] The color of this House, of which I subsequently became a member, is White. In the year of its debut (1967), the athletic House registered impressive successes in all areas of competition. The soccer team was a runner-up, the House won the table tennis senior trophy, and attained third place in volleyball competition. In the athletics meeting, the House won the Medley Relay and the tug-of-war competitions, and settled for third place at the end of the meeting. Other Houses at the time were Macauley (blue), Faduma (red), Brown-Nicols (yellow), and Greensmith (Green).

The principal worked towards the launching of the school's marching band and applied for a grant of one hundred leones (Le 100) to launch the school's band fund.[5] Efforts to launch the marching band were first made in 1962 when Mr. I. T. A. Wallace Johnson, an alumnus, donated ten pounds (£10) during a reminiscence ceremony on February 3, 1962 to start a band fund.[6] Principal Hastings-Spaine delegated the responsibility of providing the marching band to the Old Boys Association (OBA) of the Collegiate School. During the 1967/68 academic year, some musical

---

2. Interview (1984/5) with Mr. S. B. Moiba; see also Minutes of the last regular Meeting of the Board of Governors of the Collegiate School, Friday March 21, 1969.

3. See Minutes of the Board of Governors of the Collegiate School, Friday March 21, 1969.

4. *Collegiate School Diamond Jubilee Handbook 1911-1971*, 40.

5. Minutes of the Board of Governors of the Collegiate School, Friday March 21, 1969.

6. *The Collegiate School Grapevine*, May 1984, 27.

instruments that had been ordered by the OBA arrived at the school.[7] However, the instruments lay idle for over fourteen years while the band fund continued to be functional. In January 1970, the OBA contributed fifty leones (Le 50) to the fund.[8]

Principal Hastings-Spaine (hereinafter, the principal) had to enforce some disciplinary standards during his administration. Yet disciplinary responsibilities were bifurcated or distributed between the school and parents or guardians. The school assumed responsibility for the behavior of students only when they were in school. Therefore, the school did not take responsibility for the unsatisfactory behavior of students out of its purview.[9] Apparently, the principal had a legal mind. The principal strongly felt that the Road Transport Department (RTD) should supplement the transportation of students to minimize tardiness. The new busing concept was based on his resentment of tardiness but also probably based on experiences abroad. It was abnormal practice for schools to have their own buses or for students to be bused to school. Therefore, the principal arranged with the Traffic Manager of the RTD to put RTD buses at the disposal of students.[10] Structural development was just as important as the issue of punctuality.

In 1966, the principal saw an opportunity for the construction of another building. It should be recalled that the proprietors fell short in 1961 when they were unable to allocate funds to the construction of more buildings. By 1966, the number of students on roll had increased and an adjunct building became necessary. The US Government provided funds for construction of the building but the school was responsible for the wages of construction workers.[11] The building was constructed in addition to two apartments and the building was used by fifth Formers. Pioneering co-educational business students subsequently utilized the structure in the 1980s till part of the 1990s (at least).

The principal conceptualized public events as occasions to celebrate the successes of the school. Accordingly, prize-giving ceremonies that were traditionally held on an annual basis became contingent on the academic performance of students in public exams and the quality of rehearsals for public events. Prize-giving ceremonies were not likely to be held when

7. *The Collegiate School Grapevine*, May 1984, 27.
8. Minutes of the Board of Governors of the Collegiate School, Tuesday June 30, 1970.
9. The Collegiate School Reports, 1969 and 1970.
10. The Collegiate School Reports, 1969 and 1970.
11. Interview (1984/5) with Mr. S. B. Moiba.

The Administration of Mr. Hastings-Spaine (1966–71)

General Certificate of Examinations (GCE) results were poor, or when students engaged in substandard rehearsals for public events.[12]

The Hastings-Spaine administration enjoyed a reasonable amount of stability and progress until 1968 when the administrative machinery started to fall apart. Problems came to the fore after the principal's arrival from Newcastle; he had just completed a Master of Education course in the United Kingdom. Prior to 1969, the finances and administration of the school were relatively sound and audited statements of the school indicated that the school was in a financially healthy position at the end of the 1967/68 academic year.[13]

Rev. V. J. Hastings-Spaine, Esq., BA, DipTh
Principal of the Collegiate School (1966–71)

When the principal went on study leave, with the approval of the BoGs, he asked Mr. A. C. Beckley, the vice principal, to act on his behalf. After December 9, 1969, when the principal returned, issues of financial irregularities and administrative problems surfaced. Articles had vanished, chairs were inadequate, and funds had been depleted.

---

12. Interview (1984/5) with Mr. S. B. Moiba.
13. Minutes of the Board of Governors of the Collegiate School, Monday October 13, 1969.

The West African Methodist Collegiate School, 1911–2021

In 1969, the sum of nine hundred and forty-eight leones (Le 948) was paid into the school's account for ninety-nine students as part of dubious transactions. The *Compagnie Française de L'Afrique Occidentale* (CFAO) (The French Company of West Africa) presented a claim for three hundred and sixty-eight leones (Le 368) worth of building materials that could not be found.[14] The vouchers and books reflected excessive spending and the deficit or arrears of the school were incredulously high. The audited statement for 1968/9 revealed that frivolous and reckless loans were made to the acting principal and some members of staff. Amounts recorded for repairs, maintenance, and miscellaneous expenditures were exorbitant or exaggerated.[15] In a squabble between the principal and acting principal, the acting principal conceded that the amount of money recorded for tuition was incredibly low and misleading.[16]

When the principal resumed office, about 300 students were turned out of school for allegedly not paying tuition.[17] Most of the students argued that they had paid their fees. Some claimed that they had paid for an entire year, while others claimed that they have paid for two terms (semesters). The students organized a massive demonstration on January 20, 1970 and marched with placards from the school to the Ministry of Education in New England. The students complained that the suspension of education was an unfair and harsh decision.[18]

Some students claimed that they paid their fees of nine leones and forty cents (Le 9.40c) per term plus an additional one leone (Le 1) for stationary to the acting principal but received only temporary receipts. Others claimed that they did not receive any receipt.[19] Enraged students went to an unfinished house that the acting principal was constructing and caused considerable damage to the windows of the unfinished house.[20] Morale in the school was conspicuously low.

---

14. Minutes of the Board of Governors of the Collegiate School, Tuesday June 30, 1970; see also the Collegiate School Reports, 1969 and 1970

15. Minutes of the Board of Governors of the Collegiate School, Monday October 13, 1969.

16. Minutes of the Board of Governors of the Collegiate School, Tuesday June 30, 1970.

17. Metzger, No title, 8.

18. Metzger, No title, 8.

19. Metzger, No title, 8.

20. Interview (1984/5) with Mr. S. B. Moiba.

The Administration of Mr. Hastings-Spaine (1966–71)

The unsettling contradictions and administrative acrimony within the school lingered for some time. When asked by the Ministry of Education about what should be done to resolve the discontents of the students, the principal replied that he could not assume responsibility for what he did not know.[21] Problems in the school continued to fester and the acting principal, who went on sick leave, provided no avenue for the problems to be resolved.[22] He was subsequently interdicted and asked to pay six hundred and two leones (Le 602) through the Ministry of Education in order to offset his indebtedness to the school.[23]

In 1969, the BoGs set up a committee to look into the irregularities that had caused consternation, indignation, and public discomfiture.[24] Complicating and astounding views were expressed and the acting principal was dismissed. A lot of financial leakages had taken place and it became apparent that it would cost the school one thousand leones (Le 1000) in overdraft, a considerable amount of money at the time, to meet its financial commitments.[25]

Old problems quickly resurfaced. The principal had to arrange for the purchase of forty chairs for the geography room and the library from a private company, A. Genet and Co. Structural plans for building staff quarters did not materialize and some actual or potential teachers were not able to benefit from housing facilities. However, the student population was kept stable at about 500 students to stabilize the structural problems.[26] One hundred and twenty students were admitted into the school in September 1970.[27] One hundred and eight students were placed in Forms 1A, B, and C; Form 1D was reserved for students who were held back (repeaters). The remaining twelve students were admitted into Forms 2 and 3. No new student was admitted into Form 4 or 5. By the end of the 1969 academic year, sixty pupils were asked to leave the school because of performance-related issues (about 480 students were enrolled at the time).[28]

---

21. Metzger, No title, 8.
22. Labor, No title, 46.
23. The Collegiate School Reports, 1969 and 1970.
24. Labor, No title, 46.
25. Minutes of the Board of Governors of the Collegiate School, Monday October 13, 1969.
26. The Collegiate School Reports, 1969 and 1970.
27. The Collegiate School Reports, 1969 and 1970.
28. Minutes of the Board of Governors of the Collegiate School, Thursday November 5, 1970.

While the school was adequately staffed for some subjects in 1971, the school had difficulties recruiting graduate teachers for geography, biology, and chemistry.[29] There were only ten graduate teachers, five Teachers with Advanced Certificates (TAC), and four with General Certificate of Education (GCE).[30] Two TAC teachers, Mrs. Erica Roy-Macauley and Mr. S. T. Lewis-Nicol, left for a general degree course at Fourah Bay College (FBC). Miss Stanella Beckley left for a five-year course in France.

During the Hastings-Spaine administration, staffing problems were largely connected with inadequate residential accommodations. Staff quarters were considered to be an enticing provision to recruit and retain teachers.[31] However, some new teachers were promoted. Mr. S. B. Moiba, BA, DipEd was promoted to the position of Senior Teacher, effective September 1970, to replace Mr. Beckley. Miss Olive Johnson, BA, DipEd was appointed Senior Teacher "Internal," effective January 1, 1971.

Student promotion was based on annual academic performance (unlike the criterion in 1911). There were terminal examinations and students had to score a minimum of 45 percent to be promoted.[32] The inherited British standard of evaluation had a deflationary twist that was extended to the University of Sierra Leone. The deflated standard of evaluation caused (and still causes) problems with international competitiveness. Students of Forms 1 to 3 who fell short of the standard may be reconsidered under extenuating circumstances, recommendations by teachers. Mitigating conditions did not apply to students of the fourth Form.[33]

Students were generally encouraged to study liberal arts and science subjects, and provisions were also made for students to study accounting, commerce, shorthand, typing (word processing), and French. Students who chose to study typing were required to pay an additional two leones (Le 2) per term. Typing was not made available to students of Forms 1 and 2.[34]

29. Minutes of the Board of Governors of the Collegiate School, Thursday November 5, 1970.

30. Minutes of the Board of Governors of the Collegiate School, Thursday November 5, 1970.

31. Minutes of the Board of Governors of the Collegiate School, Thursday November 5, 1970.

32. Principal Hastings-Spaine, in Minutes of the Board of Governors, "Handing Over Notes," 5 November, 1970.

33. Principal Hastings-Spaine, in Minutes of the Board of Governors, "Handing Over Notes," 5 November, 1970.

34. Principal Hastings-Spaine, in Minutes of the Board of Governors, "Handing Over

The Administration of Mr. Hastings-Spaine (1966–71)

From 1966 to 1971, students performed reasonably well in the GCE. In 1966, ninety-three students took the GCE; seventy-nine students successfully passed at least one subject and fourteen outrightly failed. There was a spike in the number of students who attempted the examination in the 1966/67 academic year; 107 students attempted the examination and eighty-seven students passed at least one subject. The principal and staff were not happy about the results. The disappointing 1966/67 results forced the principal to reduce the number of students who attempted the examination the following academic year (1967/68).

In 1970, there was a subtle change in the grading pattern and name of the examination. In addition to "GCE," the examination was restructured to include a school certificate component. In the same year, the school presented twenty-four students to attempt what became known as the "School Certificate/General Certificate of Examination," the SC/GCE; nine students were unsuccessful. The following year, the number was increased to forty-seven students but only seventeen were successful. Between 1966 and 1971, government grants augmented the finances of the school and helped to prepare the students for public exams; tuition, stationary fees, sale of school colors, pupil offerings, shorthand and typing fees, and contributions by the proprietors of the school also financed the operations of the school.[35]

4.2 The Diamond Jubilee Celebrations

Preparations for the Diamond Jubilee celebrations started on Sunday May 31, 1970 when the Rev. C. O. A. Davies, MSc, LLSm (London), from the Episcopal Church of Liberia rendered a sermon in Samaria Church, located on the intersection of Siaka Stevens and Waterloo Streets, as a pre-Diamond Jubilee Discourse.[36]

The sermon was based on the book of Leviticus, chapter 25, verses 8–12, which recalled three main concepts—the Jubilee, the year of the Jubilee, and the Atonement. The multiple meanings of the word, "Jubilee," were highlighted. " During the days of Israel," he asserted, "[Jubilee] was limited to the 50th year;[37] that is, the year after the 'Seven times Seven year' period

---

Notes," 5 November, 1970.

35. Principal Hastings-Spaine, in Minutes of the Board of Governors, "Handing Over Notes," 5 November, 1970.
   36. *Collegiate Diamond Jubilee Handbook 1911–1971*, 54.
   37. *Collegiate Diamond Jubilee Handbook 1911–1971*, 55–56.

when there was to be no sowing, nor even gathering of natural products of the field and the vine." He contemporaneously recalled the varying characterizations of the word that could be associated with celebrations of twenty-fifth, fiftieth, or sixtieth anniversaries of important events. "Jubilee," he asserted, comes from an ancient Hebrew word meaning a "ram's horn" or trumpet;[38] for according to Hebrew tradition, a year of atonement and rejoicing was proclaimed every fiftieth year.

For the Collegiate School, however, June 1, 1971, marked sixty years of chequered history and what was acclaimed to be a "Diamond Jubilee." Planning the diamond jubilee celebrations actually commenced on November 5, 1970. Arrangements were made for the production of a school calendar that would depict aspects of the school's sixty years of existence. In keeping with the arrangements, plans were completed with Sierra Leone's *Daily Mail* and the sum of seventy-five leones (Le 75) was advanced for a thousand copies.[39]

The celebrations, which were conducted under the auspices of the management of the school; and the OBA involved an elaborate program, starting from May 28, 1971 to Friday December 17, 1971.[40] On Friday May 28, 1971, a broadcast talk was delivered by the Rev. E. A. E. Cole (an alumnus). Between Friday May 28, 1971 and Friday December 17, 1971, a lot of activities were scheduled, including cricket matches, a thanksgiving service, a Foundation Day service and reminiscence, musical evening, memorial service, reception, and speech day and prize-giving ceremony. Three of the most significant activities included the annual thanksgiving service, Foundation Day celebrations, and the memorial service, which was held at Tabernacle Church at 4 PM.

In commemoration of the founding of the school and the diamond jubilee celebrations, the principal, Staff, BoGs, students, and OBA held a thanksgiving service at Samaria Church. At about 2:30 PM past and present students started to congregate on the Samaria School campus at Wellington Street. By 3:15 PM, the campus was filled with past and present students, and the members of Staff of the WAM Collegiate School. At 3:20 PM, all the attendees were called to prayers, followed by a procession to Samaria Church.

The procession to the Church was led by the marching bands of St. Edward's and the Sierra Leone Grammar School. The absence of a Collegiate

---

38. *Collegiate Diamond Jubilee Handbook 1911–1971*, 55–56.

39. See Minutes of the Board of Governors of the Collegiate School, Thursday November 5, 1970.

40. *Collegiate Diamond Jubilee Handbook 1911–1971*, 63.

The Administration of Mr. Hastings-Spaine (1966-71)

School marching band should be noteworthy. Despite the efforts that were made in the 1960s to provide a marching band, the Collegiate School did not have a functional marching band at the time. The procession went down Wellington Street, turned left through Lamina Sankoh Street, and up to Samaria Church along Waterloo Street.

The preacher for the occasion was one of the distinguished alumni, the Rev. Dr. W. E. A. Pratt, OBE, MA, DD. He based his text on Acts chapter 9, verse 6, which states "Lord, what wilt thou have me to do?" and Acts chapter 2, verse 37: "What shall we do?" (see Appendix 4A). In an interesting but puzzling irony, Dr. Pratt stated that his audience was sixty years of age irrespective of whether individuals were born thirteen, fourteen, or nineteen years ago; the reason being that the experience that the school has passed on belonged to his audience by heritage.

Rev. Dr. W. E. A. Pratt, OBE, MA, DD

He drew attention to sensitive issues of the day in the country; especially education and the burning issue of unemployment. He noted that a considerable amount of emphasis should be placed on agriculture, something that Principals Macauley and Professor Faduma had stressed. He argued that agriculture provides dividend rather than dubious and ill-gotten wealth. After the thanksgiving service, students, alumni, principal and staff embarked on a much more elaborate procession.

Two distinguished alumni led the procession—the Rev. I. S. T. Fewry, who was a foundation student, and Mr. H. Ralph-James. The procession went along Siaka Stevens Street, Wellington Street, Pademba Road, Campbell Street, Sanders Street, back to Siaka Stevens Street, and finally ended at the Samaria School campus on Wellington Street. Hundreds of spectators supportively cheered the procession of the participants. It was a momentous and memorable occasion that was full of excitement and grace, befitting an institution with such a chequered history.

Foundation Day was observed on Tuesday June 1, 1971. Divine service was held in the school's chapel at 10 AM. The designated guest speaker, J. B. Fakondoh Esq., could not make it but he was deputized. Students were dismissed after the divine service and early ceremonies only to reassemble at 5 PM in the evening for the evening reminiscences and traditional distribution of pennies (cents).

Reminiscences and the traditional distribution of pennies occurred at 5 PM under the chairmanship of J. Galba-Bright, Esq., OBE, JP. The speakers for the occasion were Messrs. R. C. E. Barlatt and F. Gordon Harris. Since it was customary to not have classes on Foundation Day, classes were not held on Tuesday June 1, 1971. Freshmen were very pensive and restless about the evening ceremonies.

The format for the receipt of "pennies" was very structured. After the speakers had rendered their reminiscences, alumni and present students were invited to receive a "penny" each. The format was that the alumni would first walk up to the dais in the assembly hall, shake hands with the Chairman of the occasion, collect a "penny," and move out of the hall. After the alumni had received their "pennies," members of staff would be called upon to collect their "pennies," followed by students in the order of seniority (Forms 5 to 1).

An amazing characteristic of the "pennies" is that they were always glittering as if they had been newly minted. Notably, that had always been the case since the commencement of the ceremony during the Old Collegiate

The Administration of Mr. Hastings-Spaine (1966–71)

School of 1911.[41] Actually, "pennies" had been discontinued by the time of the event and were considered to be "cents" in 1971. Notwithstanding, the ceremonial essence of the event made the retirement of the "pennies" and the use of cents a difference without distinction. A simple rationale for understanding the concept of the tradition is that the number of pennies that were received over time indicated the length of years that one had spent at the school. It is not very apparent why there was a preference for glittering "pennies." One could only surmise that the "pennies" symbolized the uniqueness of the circumstances for which they were issued.

At the end of reminiscent ceremonies, freshmen were informally initiated by the senior or older students. The freshmen would take a whipping on their way home as a rite of passage to becoming integral members of the Collegiate School. When the author of this book became a freshman, he was very lucky to have escaped the intolerable punishment unscathed by using some very obscure routes (*"bush road"*) to get home. In a remarkable twist of coincidence or happenstance, he also escaped similar punishment when he got to Fourah Bay College. Less adroit and unlucky students who lived in the city (Freetown) and elsewhere were not so lucky to evade the brutal punishment after receiving the traditional pennies and participating in some good laughs of reminiscence. A memorial service followed the occasion.

Sunday June 27, 1971, was set aside for those who had made outstanding contributions to the development of the school. A memorial service was held at Tabernacle Church, Circular Road, at 4 PM and the preacher was the Rev. E. A. E. Cole. His text was from Zachariah chapter 1, verse 5, which reads: "Your fathers, where *are* they? And the prophets, do they live forever?"[42] The purpose of the text was to show that man is a pilgrim or sojourner on earth. Pointedly, man's nature on earth is transient:

> Man has no stay in life. He has only to make good of the opportunity that comes to him, time after time. He has to make his own contribution, in his own way, to the building up of the world and the society in which he lives. It is true man comes, and man goes, and like a bubble on the stream on which for a few passing moments the light and shadows play and then he is forgotten like a dream, dies at the opening day.[43] (Rev. E. A. E. Macauley)

---

41. Interview (1984/5) with Mr. T. W. Clarkson.
42. *Collegiate Diamond Jubilee Handbook 1911–1971*, 74.
43. *Collegiate Diamond Jubilee Handbook 1911–1971*, 74.

The Rev. Macauley paid special tribute to the early principals and acting principals of the school by recounting their great deeds. He also paid homage to some alumni of the school such as Mr. I. T. A. Wallace Johnson; Mr. Ahmed Alahdi, MBE, who had been Master and Registrar of the Supreme Court in Sierra Leone; Mr. J. T. Harding, BA (Durham University), and Dr. J. B. Fashole-Luke. Students were cautioned to take their work seriously in order to put Collegiate School on the map of education. The Rev. Macauley ended his sermon with some prayerful words:

> When the day of toil is done,
> When the race of life is run,
> Father, grant thy wearied one
> Rest for evermore. (John Ellerton, 1870)

At the end of the service, past and present students, and representatives of the WAM church joined in a procession to lay wreaths on the grave of the late Rev. John Brown-Nicols (former General Superintendent of the WAM church and acting principal) at Circular Road. Mr. Crispin George composed an ode as a contribution to the Diamond Jubilee celebrations. The ode consists of four verses and the fourth has been reproduced for ease of reference:[44]

> Our School is threescore year today
> Rah! Rah! Collegiate Rah!
> Father remain her guide and stay;
> Rah! Rah! Collegiate Rah!
> With thee her arm shall never fall,
> Be thou her guiding star;
> Thus shall she evermore prevail;
> Rah! Rah! Collegiate Rah! (Crispin George, 1971)

On Thursday July 22, 1971, the OBA of the school held a grand reception in honor of two distinguished alumni, the Rev. I. S. T. Fewry and Mr. J. Galba-Bright for the award of the Officer of the Order of the British Empire (OBE). The reception was part of the jubilee celebrations and a gift was presented to the outgoing principal, Mr. Hastings-Spaine.

---

44. *Collegiate Diamond Jubilee Handbook 1911–1971*, 78.

The Administration of Mr. Hastings-Spaine (1966–71)

4.3 The Final Days of the Hastings-Spaine Administration

The principal spent the final days dealing with the finances of the school as a result of the irregularities that were foisted upon him. The financial anomalies had created problems in 1969 but the principal was able to bring about a successful restoration of the finances of the school by 1971.

Between 1970 and 1971, readjustments were made to the school's student population. In the 1969/70 academic year seventy students were asked to leave the school and in September 1970, 120 students had been admitted. By so doing, the principal reduced the population of the school relative to the time when he assumed office. Consequently, the population of the school by the end of 1971 was 478.

Two unfortunate incidents dogged the Hastings-Spaine administration, the financial and administrative problems that destabilized the structural plans for improvement of the school. As a result, ambitious physical projects remained unattainable. While the Collegiate School faced problems in the 1970s, problems were also developing at the CMS Grammar School.

The principal of the Grammar School, the Rev. L. O. Palmer, was planning to retire and take a position as Dean at the St. George's Cathedral after serving the Grammar School for six years.[45] Mr. Hastings-Spaine decided to move over to the Grammar School, his alma mater, when the vacancy for a principal opened up in 1971. The Collegiate School was informed of the impending leadership vacuum in 1970/71 and the school had to search for a replacement principal one more time. Mr. L. B. Rogers-Wright replaced Mr. Hastings-Spaine.

---

45. King, "History of the Sierra Leone Grammar School," 124.

5

The Administration of Principal Rogers-Wright (1971–78)

AFTER THE RESIGNATION OF Mr. Hastings-Spaine, the Board of Governors (BoGs) of the Collegiate School invited applications from the public to fill the vacancy. Applications were received from Messrs. W. O. Pratt, BSc Hons., DipEd, and L. B. Rogers-Wright, BA, DipEd to fill the vacancy. The BoGs summoned an emergency meeting after receipt of the applications at the school's library on Friday July 2, 1971, at 5:30 PM.[1]

The most important issue confronting the BoGs was the matter of leadership. After deliberations, the BoGs unanimously agreed to recommend Mr. L. B. Rogers-Wright to the Ministry of Education for the position and resolved that he be appointed principal of the school effective August 1, 1971.[2] Mr. L. B. Rogers-Wright acted as principal on a contingency basis during the 1971/72 academic year. Once again, the school had a principal who was not an alumnus of the school.

Born in 1944, Mr. Rogers-Wright started to attend the Prince of Wales (POW) in the late 1940s and got his entire secondary education (up to the sixth Form) from the POW.[3] He later earned a BA, DipEd (Durham) from Fourah Bay College (FBC) at a time when FBC was affiliated with Durham University in the United Kingdom. After graduation he started to teach

---

1. Minutes of an emergency meeting of the Board of Governors of the Collegiate School, Friday July 2, 1971.

2. Minutes of an emergency meeting of the Board of Governors of the Collegiate School, Friday July 2, 1971.

3. *Collegiate School Magazine* 6 (July 1978) 26–27.

The Administration of Principal Rogers-Wright (1971–78)

at the POW and rose to the rank of a Senior Teacher. He was placed in charge of prefects, school discipline, and the Literary and Debating Society (L&DS).[4] He became vice principal of the POW and held that position until he accepted the principalship position at the Collegiate School.

5.1 The Administration of Mr. Rogers-Wright

The administration of Mr. Rogers-Wright was similar to that of his predecessor and I actually became a student of the Collegiate School during his tenure. He continued the tradition of recruiting qualified members of staff, emphasized discipline, and protected the academic and social welfare of students by providing adequate chairs, recruiting qualified faculty members, and encouraging the development of sports and recreation. In the 1970s, the school was able to attract qualified recruits from abroad; for example, Mr. Wamadeva Balachandran, an expatriate from Ceylon (Sri Lanka; 1971),[5] was employed to help with math and science.

Approximately ten faculty members out of twenty-two had degrees with a Diploma in Education. Five had university degrees, four had teaching certificates, one had a Diploma in Engineering, one had a BA (Inter.) from London, and one had GCE A Level. The school lost a long-serving faculty member, Mr. D. C. Thomas, to retirement.[6] It should be recalled that Mr. D. C. Thomas was part of the staff who resuscitated the school in 1948. By the time of his retirement in 1974, Mr. D. C. Thomas (*Master, Master*) had served the school for twenty-six years and he was a very inspirational Bible knowledge (BK) and Latin teacher.

Mr. Thomas taught Latin and BK up to the Third Form, and I was very fortunate to have him as a Latin teacher. To cause distraction, some students (bullies) exploited his gullibility by telling outlandish and horrific stories that were false because they did not want to learn Latin and BK. Given the exaggerated weight of the horrific stories, Mr. Thomas would be so appalled that he would reply, "*Lord have mercy!*" Obviously, the bullies deliberately created distractions for as long as they could because they had no interest in learning Latin or BK and relied on the acquiescence of the rest of the class. They actually relished the excitement that was derived

---

4. *The Collegiate School Magazine* 6 (July 1978) 26–27.

5. Minutes of an emergency meeting of the Board of Governors of the Collegiate School, Friday July 2, 1971.

6. *The Collegiate School Magazine* 1 (June 1973) 3.

from Mr. Thomas's responses. The repetitive nature of the distractions occasionally became too obvious and Mr. Thomas would cut them off. The members of staff organized a formal retirement celebration for Mr. Thomas and provided him gifts for his service to the school.

Strong disciplinary measures were implemented by Principal Rogers-Wright. Students who did not conform to the rules and regulations of the school (nonconformists) were severely punished in front of the school as a deterrent. However, there were repeat offenders who consistently incurred the wrath of the principal. Periodically, students will be dismissed for repetitively engaging in very bad behaviors. Others will be detained after school to perform menial cleaning jobs around the campus for a period of about three hours if they engaged in minor infractions that could not be elevated to the level of severity.

The principal was a very agile and extraordinary man. On one occasion, he got into the car of a complaining neighbor who had been tormented by students after school. Some students were in the habit of unlawfully harvesting his mangoes by dangerously throwing stones at ripe mangoes; some of the students even got gashes on their heads with blood flowing down their uniforms in the frantic effort to harvest ripe mangoes. To disguise himself, the principal asked the neighbor to get him from the school to the crime scene. He then rode with the complaining neighbor to the crime scene, which was notoriously known as "*Dooo Dooo*," a venue where students settled scores and engaged in all kinds of truancies and hanky-panky. The venue was replete with all kinds of fresh fruits and very attractive for its natural landscape and fauna.

The principal and the complaining neighbor rode right into the midst of the inattentive students and the principal got out of the car to give chase to the students who ran like sprinting rabbits. Unfortunately, some students left their books and book bags behind in the heat of unanticipated and spontaneous confusion when they realized that the principal was chasing students. The principal was very athletic, but it was an unusual and dangerously audacious move to chase students into the bushes; needless to say that the students who were caught, including those who left their books behind, got into a lot of trouble. It was very apparent that the principal had a towering and intimidating presence. Some of the culprits were punished mildly, but repeat offenders or very troublesome students were harshly expelled.

Occasional dismissals generated variations in the student population from time to time; for example, the total number of registered students was

The Administration of Principal Rogers-Wright (1971–78)

420 at the beginning of the 1972/3 academic year, but the number of the students the by the end of October that academic year dropped to 381. The number declined even further to 362 by the end of the academic year.[7] The principal observed:

> We have laid emphasis on discipline as we believe like John Milton the British 17th century writer and philosopher, that whatever power or sway in mortal things weaker men have attributed to fortune, I dur'st with more confidence ascribe hither to vigour or slackness of discipline.[8]

Lewellyn Rogers-Wright, BA (Dun.)
Principal of the Collegiate School (1971–78)

The Rogers-Wright administration also tried to stabilize the student-teacher ratio to maintain a student population that commensurate with the structural capacity of the buildings and available faculty members

---

7. The Collegiate School Report for the period covering December 1972 to November 1973.
8. L. B. Rogers-Wright in *The Collegiate School Magazine* 1 (June 1973) 13.

of the school. In his School Report for the period covering December 1972 to November 1973, Mr. Rogers-Wright observed: "The buildings as at present can be utilized to their optimum if staff is available." Faculty, structural capacity, and critical thinking skills became the hallmarks of the principal's administration.

Critical thinking skills were encouraged by the revitalization of the L&DS. Of course, the school had a long experience with the L&DS dating back to the Old Collegiate School. The society had fallen into disuse for approximately five years.[9] The L&DS was a forum for intellectual or scholarly debates among the seniors (fourth and fifth Form students) and it was placed under the supervision of Messrs. Abisodun Wilson, BA, and Mr. Abage. After its restitution. Mr. Abisodun Wilson also worked for the Sierra Leone Broadcasting Service (SLBS) and taught English literature. He taught some of us Shakespeare's *Henry V* but he would occasionally inform me that I was too young for his literature class, which was full of older students; some of whom had been held back. Some of the older and bigger boys (repeaters) surreptitiously taunted some of the older teachers by calling them names and throwing pebbles at the blackboard when the backs of the teachers faced the classroom. Evidently, some of the bullies had no interest in learning and would rather cause entertaining distractions for as long as they could.

Mr. Wilson's rendition of Act 3 Scene 1 of *Henry V* is particularly memorable and irresistible. King Henry felt that the resounding noise of war should induce his men to imitate the action of a tiger and fight without any breach of the national courage. Though they could be expected to show modest stillness and humility in times of peace, the noise of war should stiffen their sinews and summon their blood:

> Once more unto the breach, dear friends, once more;
> Or close the wall up with our English dead.
> In peace there's nothing so becomes a man
> As modest stillness and humility:
> But when the blast of war blows in our ears,
> Then imitate the action of the tiger;
> Stiffen the sinews, summon up the blood,
> Disguise fair nature with hard-favour'd rage.[10]

---

9. *The Collegiate School Magazine* 1 (June 1973) 13.
10. Shakespeare, *Henry V*, 3.1.1–8.

The Administration of Principal Rogers-Wright (1971-78)

The L&DS met mainly on Friday afternoons and the principal would episodically explain the importance of the society to the senior students. The society had about eighty members in 1974.[11] The governing body of the L&DS was a management committee, which consisted of eight members and a disciplinary committee of six members, consisting of the Chief Whip (the Senior Prefect). I found the L&DS to be very interesting and fruitful though I was more of an observer. It was one of the few organizations in the school that could boast of animated exchange of ideas across a spectrum of issues.

It was common to have debates, impromptu speeches, and quizzes. As a freshman, I recall quietly watching the procession of the seniors to the assembly hall for L&DS meetings. Though I was very curious to know what was going on in the meetings, I did not have a glimpse until I became a member in 1976. In the late 1970s, the eclectic programs of the L&DS were supervised by Mr. S. T. Lewis-Nicol, BA, DipEd.

Some students of other secondary schools in close proximity to the Collegiate School, such as the Grammar School, Prince of Wales, and St. Joseph's Convent, were occasionally invited to participate in the L&DS meetings. Music-loving students who were also partly responsible for drawing up L&DS programs would include the discussion of pop music in the programs. Some of the senior students acted as pop jurors. Invariably, I looked forward to the L&DS meetings because of the excitement and learning experience that it provided. Scouting also gained a new lease on life during the administration of Principal Rogers-Wright. Recall that students of the Old Collegiate School enjoyed some scouting and hiking to distant villages and venues. The enthusiasm was not any different in the 1970s.

In 1974, the Scout Guild of the school was resurrected after a period of abeyance (about four to five years) as the 16th Freetown Troop.[12] The Physical Education teacher, Mr. M. M. T. Coker, was placed in charge of the Troop. Mr. H. Sankoh, the Physics Laboratory Assistant, became the Assistant Scoutmaster. However, towards the end of the Rogers-Wright administration, Mr. Sankoh became the Scout Master of the Troop. The Scout Master, Coker, had been dismissed by the principal. Other officials of the troop included: George Hedd-Williams, leader of the Wolf Patrol; Moses Lake, the leader of the Lion Patrol; Francis Parsons (an outstanding athlete

---

11. *The Collegiate School Magazine* 1 (June 1973) 13.
12. *The Collegiate School Magazine* 3 (November 1975) 13.

and soccer player), leader of the Tiger Patrol; Misbow Dumbuya, leader of the Panther Patrol; and Muminie Thomas, Leader of the Dragon Patrol.[13]

Incidentally, I became a member of the Dragon Patrol and subsequently became a leader of the Patrol. Scouting activities were very ambitious and challenging but exciting. Scouts took part in hikes, camps, and award schemes. Between 1974 and 1978, scouting constituted an exquisite addition to extracurricular activities of the school. The principal was also interested in a streamlined curriculum.

Immediately after taking office, teachers were asked to develop syllabi that were unique to the levels of courses taught at the school; each department created a committee in that regard. The nature of the syllabi reflected academic training and exposure to external seminars and conferences.[14] Teachers were asked to write weekly, monthly, and terminal forecasts to ensure comprehensive and structured teaching. The principal was also interested in his own professional development.

Four years after his appointment, Mr. Rogers-Wright decided to undertake a Diploma in Advanced Studies in Education and a Master of Education from the University of Bristol. Mr. S. B. Moiba, BA, DipEd (Dunelm), who was vice principal, acted as principal. Mr. Moiba was born in Baiama Town, Tankoro Chiefdom in Kono District in 1934. He started to obtain preliminary education in 1938. He was given the name Solomon by his benefactor, the Rev. Canon Theo. E. Harding.[15]

Mr. Moiba started his education at the WAM Collegiate School in February 1952, after which he went to Fourah bay College in 1958 to earn a BA, DipEd in June 1966. He joined the faculty of the Collegiate School in 1966 and became a Senior Teacher in 1970. The position was officially recognized by the Ministry of Education in September 1972 after he completed a year's educational administration course in the UK.[16]

Mr. Moiba received official handover notes from Mr. Rogers-Wright in August 1975. During Mr. Moiba's tenure, the Parent Teacher Association (PTA) became a reliable partner in the matters of the school. The PTA had hitherto been of insignificant value[17] but Mr. Moiba was determined

---

13. *The Collegiate School Magazine* 3 (November 1975) 13.
14. *The Collegiate School Magazine* 1 (June 1973) 28.
15. Interview (1985) with Mr. S. B. Moiba.
16. Interview (1985) with Mr. S. B. Moiba.
17. Interview (1985) with Mr. S. B. Moiba; see also Minutes of an Emergency Meeting of the Board of Governors of the Collegiate School, December 3, 1971.

The Administration of Principal Rogers-Wright (1971-78)

to make it more useful. He had observed the effectiveness of PTAs in foreign countries when he was abroad and he had realized the beneficial contributions that PTAs could make to the advancement of schools.[18]

The educational administrative course in the United Kingdom (1971/2) gave Mr. Moiba an opportunity to observe the efficacy of a PTA. He was attached to the Cherwell Secondary School and the PTA of the school made financial contributions toward the construction of a swimming pool for the school. More inspiring was a picture that appeared in a local newspaper, *The Oxford Times*, in which the principal, Mr. Baldwin, was in his swimming suit and surrounded by students of the school. The resonance of such an experience was aptly summed up:

> If a developed country like the UK can rely on a PTA to help the School to provide what the Government cannot do or cannot provide, it is more necessary for an underdeveloped country to have a strong PTA than can help the School financially in times of need.[19]

In 1975, the first PTA meeting was summoned and officials were elected. Mr. J. R. Thorpe (the author's grandfather and retired Inspector of Prisons) was elected to be the President of the organization, Mrs. C. B. Cole, a primary school teacher, was elected to be treasurer and Miss. M. A. Williams (later Mrs. Macauley, one of the author's history teachers), was elected to be secretary. The turnout for the very first meeting was rather discouraging but not crippling.

Mr. Moiba developed a clever ruse to reinforce the importance of PTA meetings on the minds of parents and students. Students' whose parents or guardians did not attend the meeting (the rollout of the organization) were sent home to ensure that their parents or guardians met with the acting principal on the following morning. The insistence generated an unmistakable clarity about the importance of PTA meetings and the organization subsequently made significant contributions to the development of the school.

The acting principal got help from the Chairman of the school's prize-giving ceremony on December 12, 1975, Dr. Ivan O. Findlay, who emphasized the importance of the PTA. The Chairman directed attention to the fact that some schools are badly clad for educational purposes and that there is a vital role for PTAs in the development of secondary schools.

---

18. Interview (1985) with Mr. S. B. Moiba.
19. Interview (1985) with Mr. S. B. Moiba.

Some of the schools had poor educational facilities and were conspicuously congested. The Chairman noted:

> PTAs in the advanced countries, with education budgets less than those of developing nations have been able to do something. . . . PTAs have lobbied members of Parliament to such an extent that . . . conditions were improved upon. . . . PTAs can assist a school educationally, socially, and financially. [20]

After stabilizing the PTA, the acting principal delegated some responsibilities to the PTA; for example, the PTA was asked to pay for one of the marching bands that performed in the 1976 thanksgiving service. By 1976, the Collegiate School was still without a marching band. The PTA was also financially responsible for the refreshments of the cast, school's choir, and the members of the scout troop after the thanksgiving ceremony in December 1976. The PTA also issued prizes for punctuality, which the author won for three years (1972–75). Prizes for writing (to minimize bad penmanship) and athletics (best athlete) were also provided by the PTA. The PTA effectively became important not only for discussing the academic performance of students and social behaviors in the school but for assisting with essential financial capital to augment the expenditures of the school.[21]

The PTA soon realized its integral role in the development of the school. Accordingly, it elevated its role and importance to the school. Each member of the PTA was asked to make financial contributions to a newly established PTA Fund, which was opened in one of the banks of Sierra Leone. Hence, the PTA played a pivotal role in the operations of the school during the tenure of Mr. Moiba. As the PTA increased its public profile, attention was also directed to curriculum diversification.

A new course in business methods was added to the school's curriculum for fourth and fifth Formers who were incapable of coping with either Latin or French (foreign languages). However, 1975 proved to be one of the most difficult years to recruit and retain faculty members.[22] The reliance on part-time teachers for mathematics and physics was problematic. Additionally, a music teacher, Mr. A. O. Smith (who taught at the school for fourteen years, including while the author was at the school), also retired. He was a source of amusement for some students; John Maclean, an exceptionally talented javelinist of national acclaim comes to mind.

20. Dr. I. O. Findlay in *Collegiate School Magazine* 4 (July 1976) 43.
21. Interviews (1985) with Messrs. J. R. Thorpe and S. B. Moiba.
22. *The Collegiate School Magazine* 4 (July 1976) 17.

The Administration of Principal Rogers-Wright (1971–78)

Some students would occasionally, repeatedly, and indignantly or annoyingly shout his first name, *Albaya! Albaya! Albaya!* ... to see his sudden reaction and gestures of disapproval. Students, especially junior students, could not rat out offenders for fear of retaliation by bullies; rats run the risk of being assaulted and losing their lunches. Mr. Smith was a valuable member of the school and he was responsible, together with Miss Hunter (Mrs. Wilson), for grooming the school's choir and the entire school for special occasions like prize-giving ceremonies and thanksgiving services. It was inexcusable for students to not know how to sing the school's song. Students will be held back for rehearsals until they can demonstrate satisfactory performances.

A soccer competition was organized to celebrate the retirement of Mr. Smith. The commemorative match was between female and male faculty members. However, students were asked to perform the role of goalkeepers. The male faculty members had their hands tied behind their backs while the females were permitted to play unimpeded (see Table 5.1 for participants).

Table 5.1: Players of the Commemorative Soccer Competition in Honor of Mr. Smith

Male Participants	Female Participants
Mr. S. T. Lewis-Nicol	Miss. H. A. Hooke (Mrs. Kawaley)
Mr. D. B. Amara	Mrs. G. B. Tucker
Mr. V. Balaranjan	Mrs. M. A. Macauley
Mr. T. J. Cole	Mrs. A. P. Hazema-Wilson
Mr. A. A. Martyn (physical education teacher)	Miss. G. K. Thomas

Mr. A. O. Smith took the kickoff and the match started accordingly. The exhilarating match lasted for ten minutes and it gave students a very rare opportunity to see some of the unfamiliar human attributes of their faculty members. It was a very funny occasion that was filled with short-lived laughter and cheers; many wanted a prolonged action beyond the ten-minute duration of the match. Importantly, the gesture was more meaningful and highly appreciated. Interestingly, the match ended in an unexpected draw (1–1), which seemed to be very unusual but seemingly fit for the occasion; it looked like the fix was in for a fitting resolution of a competition that honored the academic contributions of a very interesting faculty member.

The composition of the contestants of the commemorative match was also revealing of gender diversification in the mid 1970s. When the school was originally established, it was made up of male teachers. In 1948, the faculty consisted of no female teacher. Between the end of 1974 and the end of 1977, the school had an impressive number of female teachers. Some of the teachers were recruited between December 1976 and November 1977.

While the acting principal was busy modifying the curriculum and diversifying the faculty, thieves started to burglarize the school. In December 1976, some science equipments were stolen from the physics laboratory. The Grammar School had witnessed similar occurrences in the past. Chairs mysteriously disappeared from the Collegiate School. The acting principal called on the Criminal Investigation Department (CID) of the country to promptly investigate the theft.

Diligent investigations were conducted and some of the equipments were recovered. It turned out that one of the laboratory assistants was responsible for the theft. Indeed, stealing constituted one of the most serious problems of the Moiba administration, and it was one of those problems that did not augur well for the administration of the school. Just at about the time when Principal Rogers-Wright was about to return from study leave, thieves stole the battery of Mr. Moiba's car.

The escalating levels of theft created animosity between the acting principal and the BoGs, and the animosity is arguably one of the reasons why Mr. Moiba never became principal of the school. Embattled by the levels of theft at the school, the acting principal experimented with *black magic* to identify the thieving culprit(s). The BoGs viewed the incident with disapproval and consternation. The traditional practice unequivocally clashed with the religious mission of the school and members of the BoGs were unhappy. It is evident that Mr. Moiba was extremely frustrated by the recurrence of theft at the school, but the preferred remedy proved to be stunning and inappropriate to the BoGs.

The Administration of Principal Rogers-Wright (1971–78)

Table 5.2 A Cross-section of Teachers at the Collegiate School (1974–77)φ

Male Faculty Members	Female Faculty Members
Mr. S. T. Lewis-Nicol, BA, DipEd	Miss. G. K. Thomas, HTC
Mr. A. G. Panda, BA, DipEd	Mrs. L. M. Jaia, BSc, DipEd
Mr. H. E. P. Musah, BA	Mrs. Emma Leigh, BA (French, from abroad)*
Mr. V. Sivanathan, BSc	Mrs. Jacqueline Leigh (BA in linguistics from the United States)*
Mr. Keturay Turay, BA, DipEd*	Miss. Lois Thompson*
Mr. S. M. Swarray, BA Hons. (Econ.)*	Miss. H. A. Hooke (Mrs. Kawaley), BA, DipEd
Mr. P. Jesudasan BA Hons., MA (Hons.)*	Mrs. G. B. Tucker
Mr. V. E. A. Green, BA Hons.*	Mrs. M. A. Macauley, BA, DipEd
Mr. E. Sam, HTC*	Mrs. A. P. Hazema-Wilson
Mr. S. A. Sesay, GCE A Level*	Miss. G. K. Thomas

φ *Qualifications of Miss. G. K. Thomas, Mrs A. P. Hazema-Wilson, Mrs. G. B. Tucker, and Miss Lois Thompson could not be obtained; see also the* Collegiate School Magazine, *July 1976, 4:17.*

* *Recruited between December 1976 and November 1977.*

The chasm between the BoGs and the acting principal grew deeper and wider when for the first time in the history of the school no marching band was available for the school's thanksgiving service just before the return of the principal in 1977.[23] The incident was an unmitigated disaster and embarrassment for the school. It is extremely difficult to surmise or characterize the unusual twist of events during the Moiba administration, but one could

---

23. Interview (1985) with Mr. S. B. Moiba.

be easily inclined to think that an inordinate amount of effort was made to sabotage his administration and demonstrably ensure his discomfiture.

Between 1972 and 1973, the educational policies of the school led to very modest improvements in academic performance of the students who attempted the SC/GCE Exams (see Figure 6.1). In 1971/2, twenty-five out of the fifty-five students who took the SC/GCE failed the exam. The failure was reversed in 1972/3 when about 67 percent of those who attempted the exam became successful. The number of those attempting the exams was drastically reduced from fifty-five to twenty-seven. The following year only six students failed. In 1975, nine students out of twenty-five were unsuccessful. In 1978, I successfully passed history with distinction and successfully secured four additional passes that gave me a ticket to the prestigious Albert Academy for sixth Form education; the only individual to have been so successful that year. Additional plans were made to further the structural development of the school.

Among other things, plans for a music and art room were proposed during the Rogers-Wright administration, amounting to ten thousand leones (Le 10,000). Other proposals included the painting of the classroom building, estimated to be five thousand leones (Le 5,000), and the construction of an additional floor to the classroom building, which was estimated to be thirty five thousand six hundred and sixty-six leones (Le 35,666); pittances by today's inflationary cost of doing business. Unfortunately, the plans succumbed to natural deaths.

On January 3, 1978, the principal returned from his studies abroad. A handing over (transition) was effected before the school reopened for the second term. The principal tendered his resignation to the BoGs, which became effective on May 31, 1978, shortly after his resumption of office.[24] It is not very apparent why there was such a sudden and dramatic turn of events, but the irregularities that had plagued the school before his return could not possibly be discounted. Mr. Rogers-Wright ultimately assumed a lucrative position at Aureol Tobacco Company (ATC) (where I subsequently did internship as a student of FBC, thanks to the Student Union President, Daniel Kamara, OKama). The BoGs had to find a Caretaker principal in the person of Mr. B. A. King.

---

24. Minutes of the Collegiate School Board of Governors, May 19, 1978.

The Administration of Principal Rogers-Wright (1971-78)

5.2 A Leadership Turmoil (1978-80)

The BoGs accepted the resignation of Mr. Rogers-Wright in extenuating circumstances to be effective from May 31, 1978.[25] The resignation had been a sudden occurrence. In a letter dated April 17, 1978, addressed to the Permanent Secretary of the Ministry of Education, the Secretary of the BoGs (i.e. the principal) forwarded a draft announcement of the vacancy. An amended draft was approved and returned to the principal on May 9, 1978. The announcement for the vacancy was later published in local newspapers, *We Yone* and the *Daily Mail*. The closing date for the receipt of applications was set for June 9, 1978. Announcements were also made for the post of vice principal. The Ministry of Education approved a draft copy of the announcement on April 6, 1978. The approved drafts were published in three issues of *We Yone*, *Sunday We Yone*, and the *Daily Mail*.[26]

The BoGs received six applications for the position. The six applicants were:

1. Mr. S. T. Lewis Nicol, TAC (1963), Diploma in English (1968), BA, DipEd (FBC, 1975), Senior Teacher at the WAM Collegiate School, with three years of post graduate teaching experience;

2. Mr. Emile Lisk, BSc (Dun., 1967), PGLE (Bath, 1972), MSc (FBC, 1977), Senior Teacher at Sierra Leone Grammar School, with eleven years of post-graduate teaching experience;

3. Mr. S. B. Moiba, BA, DipEd (Dun., 1966), Senior Teacher at the WAM Collegiate School, with twelve years of post-graduate teaching experience at the WAM Collegiate School;

4. Mr. W. O. Pratt, BSc (Hons) (Dun., 1959), DipEd (Dun., 1961), vice principal, Methodist Boys High School, with seventeen years of post-graduate teaching experience;

5. Mr. Z. Smith, BA, DipEd (FBC, 1977), Senior Teacher at St. Helena Secondary School, with six years of post-graduate teaching experience; and

6. Mr. Williamson Taylor, BA (Dun., 1969), DipEd (FBC, 1970), MEd, MA, Religious Education and Comparative Religion (Howard, USA,

---

25. Minutes of the Board of Governors of the Collegiate School, May 19, 1978.

26. Appointments to Posts of Principals and Vice Principal WAM Collegiate School File (Board of Governors).

1977), Senior Teacher at Bishop Johnson Memorial School, with eight years of post-graduate teaching experience.[27]

Two of the applicants, Mr. S. T. Lewis-Nicol and Mr. S. B. Moiba, were also the only applicants for the position of vice principal. The BoGs agreed to conduct one interview. After interviewing the candidates, the members voted by secret ballot; first, for the post of principal. Mr. W. O. Pratt gained the largest number of votes, followed by a tie between Mr. Z. Smith and Mr. Williamson-Taylor. Mr. Lewis was not considered because he did not have five years of postgraduate teaching experience as required by the Ministry of Education.[28]

After the election of a principal, two motions were proposed.[29] Since Mr. Moiba was the only candidate who applied for the position of vice principal, by the process of elimination, a motion was proposed that he be appointed as vice principal. A counter motion called for the runners-up for the principalship to be considered. The counter motion prevailed by a-6 to 5 majority. Mr. Z. Smith had the larger number of votes in the contest for the position between Mr. Smith and Mr. Moiba. Accordingly, the BoGs decided to offer the position of vice principal to Mr. Z. S. F. Smith (Rev. Canon Z. S. F. Smith) and recommended Mr. W. O. Pratt and Mr. Z. S. F. Smith to the Ministry of Education as principal and vice principal respectively.

However, the Ministry of Education rejected the appointment of Mr. W. O. Pratt as principal. The BoGs had to convince Mr. Rogers-Wright to stay as a caretaker principal with a monthly honorarium as a percentage of his basic salary to incentive him to stay till the end of the academic year.[30] The members of the BoGs were actually disinclined to give the former acting principal, Mr. S. B. Moiba, a chance. There had been deep-seated animosity between the BoGs and Mr. Moiba. In a letter dated September 12, 1978, and addressed to the Minister of Education, the Board noted: "Mr. Moiba had acted as principal of the School . . . his performance in his acting capacity had not proved satisfactory to the Board." The Board was clearly not willing to install Mr. Moiba as head of the school.

---

27. Appointments to Posts of Principals and Vice Principal WAM Collegiate School File (Board of Governors).

28. Ministry of Education rules, contained in the Ministry Circular Ref. M.E.(E) 304/Vol. II/61 of August 20, 1975. See also letter from the Ministry of Education, Ref. No. ME (EA) 7/Vol. II/340, November 20, 1978.

29. In the United States, to table a motion means to postpone or suspend a motion.

30. Minutes of the Board of Governors of the Collegiate School, June 30, 1978.

The Administration of Principal Rogers-Wright (1971–78)

As tension mounted over the leadership of the school, the BoGs sought to expand its pool of candidates for the position. Mr. B. A. King, BA, DipEd, and retired principal of Freetown Teachers College (FTC), was influenced by the Board to head the school. Mr. King had a long historical affiliation with the school since the 1940s after the school was reopened at Circular Road. He was also disappointed that he was bypassed when Mr. Hastings-Spaine was given the leadership position of the school. Notwithstanding, he was persuaded to lead the school.

A delegation of the BoGs met with the Minister of Education and, according to a letter dated September 15, 1978, the selection of Mr. King as caretaker principal of the school was approved. The school, which had been closed down for more than a week prior to the start of the 1978/9 academic year was finally reopened and on September 18, 1978, Mr. B. A. King became a caretaker principal of the Collegiate School.

The tenuous situation in the school meant that new searches for leadership positions had to be conducted. The Ministry of Education directed the BoGs to re-announce the positions for leadership of the school no later than the end of the 1978/9 academic year. The BoGs re-advertised the position for principalship and by Friday July 20, 1979 applications were received from Mr. S. T. Lewis Nicol; Mr. Henry B. Fyfe, BA, DipEd; Mr. S. B. Moiba; Mrs. Louisa Pessima, BA, DipEd; Rev. Z. S. F. Smith; and Mr. Emile Lisk.[31] The applicants were interviewed in alphabetical order on Friday, July 20, 1979. Rev. Z. S. F. Smith emerged victorious after voting by secret ballot.

Accordingly, Rev. Z. S. F. Smith was recommended to the Ministry of Education but his recommendation was surprisingly rejected by the Ministry of Education. It would seem as if the Ministry had a preference. The Board was asked to advertise the position once again. Between April and May 1980, the BoG announced vacancy for the principalship position in *We Yone*.[32] Five candidates, who had previously applied, responded to the announcement: Mr. S. B. Moiba, Mr. S. T. Lewis Nicol, Mr. H. B. Fyfe, Mr. E. Lisk, and Rev. Z. S. F. Smith.[33] The Chairman of the BoGs, Brigadier J. S. Momoh, who subsequently became Major General and Head of State, elicited secret ballots after an interview of the candidates on June 2, 1980. Rev. Z. S. F. Smith emerged victorious with eight votes.[34]

31. Minutes of the Board of Governors of the Collegiate School, May 18, 1979.
32. Interview (1985) with the Rev. Z. S. F. Smith.
33. Minutes of the Board of Governors of the Collegiate School, May 30, 1980.
34. Minutes of the Board of Governors of the Collegiate School, May 30, 1980.

Prior to the meeting of June 2, 1980, the Secretary of the BoGs informed two of the applicants, Messrs. S. B Moiba and S. T. Lewis-Nicol that they will not be considered for the position of vice principal since they applied to be principal.[35] They were in effect ruled out for the position but the Secretary later reviewed and rescinded the notification.[36]

After the election of the principal, four names—Mrs. Miranda Decker, BA, DipEd; Mr. Lancelot Morgan, BA, TAC; Mr. S. B. Moiba; and Mr. S. T. Lewis-Nicol—were considered for the position of vice principal. Mr. Logan was eliminated from the process because of inadequate qualification and Mrs. M. Decker was elected for the position. The successful candidates were recommended to the Ministry of Education and this time they were confirmed. The drama came to a surprising conclusion.

5.3 The Administration of the Caretaker, Mr. B. A. King (1978–80)

Mr. B. A. King had his secondary education at the C. M. S. Grammar School from 1931 to 1935.[37] He completed his School Certificate Examination in 1935, after which he went to the FBC Teacher Training Department to complete training in teacher education. He completed his training in 1938 and started to teach at the Regent Village School. Between 1938 and 1941, the principal of the CMS Grammar School invited him to teach at the CMS Grammar School, where he taught till 1944 before obtaining a scholarship to complete a degree course at FBC. Between 1944 and 1947, he encountered difficulties with the study of geography and opted out of the course to teach at the WAM Collegiate School at Circular Road. He reentered FBC in 1957 to study history and graduated with a bachelor's degree in 1958. He spent the following year studying for a Diploma in Education (DipEd). He was principal of the Freetown Teachers College until he retired; just about the time when there was a leadership crisis at the Collegiate School in 1978.

He inherited several problems, including the inadequacy of chairs at the Collegiate School and the maintenance of the buildings. Mr. King immediately set out to repair damaged chairs and within a period of five months, students were able to get sufficient chairs. Insufficient chairs seemed to be a perennial problem in the late 1970s. The annex building for

---

35. Minutes of the Board of Governors of the Collegiate School, May 30, 1980.
36. Minutes of the Board of Governors of the Collegiate School, May 30, 1980.
37. Interview (1985) with Mr. B. A. King.

The Administration of Principal Rogers-Wright (1971–78)

the fifth Formers was badly damaged and it was excluded from the policy of restitution. The classroom was badly damaged and unsecured for desks and chairs.[38] Mr. King solicited aid from the Ministry of Education to provide 240 chairs and 280 desks from the Trade Center at Kissy Dockyard but his efforts did not materialize.[39] The principal continued the policy of gender diversification by recruiting qualified female faculty members.

By 1979, the principal secured eighteen graduate teachers and five Higher Teacher Certificate (HTC) holders. In the aggregate, there were twenty-five full time and two part-time teachers. Three of the faculty members were expatriate members for whom the school provided residential responsibilities. With a reasonably well qualified faculty, the principal was able to further diversify the school's curriculum. Commercial mathematics and statistics were added to the curriculum and Business Methods was introduced to Form 3 students. As the curriculum expanded, seating accommodations became a problem once again.

The imbalance between students and chairs resurfaced in 1979/80. In the 1978/9 academic year, each student had a seat.[40] The number of students in the following year (1979/80) increased to about 650 students with only 100 desks and chairs. Implicitly, there was only one desk and chair for every seven students.[41] The 1980 statistic is indicative of bad estimates in previous disclosures. Alternatively, a lot of chairs and tables must have disappeared between 1979 and 1980.

The incongruity between student population and seating accommodations naturally created problems. Unsurprisingly, the students revolted on January 31, 1980. Students set up barricades to the entrance of the school and the Special Security Division (SSD) had to be summoned to quell the rebellion. The SSD was notorious for its prompt and indiscriminate release of tear gas on occasions of insurrection. True to form, the officers started to indiscriminately unleash tear gas around the vicinity of the campus. The protest mushroomed as residents in close proximity became affected and infuriated. Students dashed out of the campus for the safety of their lives and belongings.[42]

38. The Collegiate School Report (1978/9).
39. Ref. No. CS9/3/Vol. I/Gen. September 24, 1979. WAM Collegiate School File. (Freetown: Ministry of Education).
40. The Collegiate School Report (1978/9).
41. The Collegiate School Report (1979/80).
42. Minutes of the Board of Governors of the Collegiate School, February 22, 1980.

The BoGs was naturally concerned about the unrest and the reasons for the agitation of the students. In the first meeting of the BoGs before the 1980 academic year, the Chairman of the Board unavoidably proposed the launching of a Commission of Inquiry to investigate the causes of the discontents on January 31, 1980.[43] It was resolved that the Board composed of Mrs. Lati-Hyde Forster (Chairwoman of the meeting), Mrs. Comfort Tom Johnson, Rev. I. S. T. Fewry, Mr. V. F. Blake, Mr. T. E. Yambasu, Mr. A. K. Fraser, Mr. B. M. Gbolie, Mr. C. A. Cole, Mr. Dan E. T. Decker, Rev. S. P. Jackson, Mr. B. A. King (the principal), Hon. A. Kabba Sei, Mr. Victor Spaine, and the Chief Education Officer (CEO) or representative of the CEO constitute itself into a Commission of Inquiry to investigate the root causes of the disturbances.[44] It became very apparent that one of the reasons for the rebellion was the lack of sufficient chairs and desks.

Students complained that sitting down on windows or leaning against walls made lessons boring. It is remarkable that the students were able to learn under such inauspicious conditions. In the 1978/79 academic year, forty-three students were enrolled for the SC/GCE; five failed completely and one did not attend. In the following year, twelve students outrightly failed out of forty-eight students who attempted the exams (see Figure 6.1). The tenure of Mr. King came to an end in 1980 and the Rev. Z. S. F. Smith became principal of the school from 1980 to 1998.

---

43. Minutes of the Board of Governors of the Collegiate School, February 22, 1980.
44. Minutes of the Board of Governors of the Collegiate School, February 22, 1980.

6

The Administration of Rev. Cannon Z. S. F. Smith (1980–98)

THE RECOMMENDATION OF THE Rev. Z. S. F. Smith to the Ministry of Education by the BoGs was rejected twice before it was confirmed. The confirmation of the Rev. Smith made him the first alumnus to head the school since its existence. Evidently, he became the principal with the longest tenure in office since the establishment of the school in 1911. However, his tenure could not outlast the civil war that gripped the country for slightly over a decade.

The Rev. Smith attended various schools in Freetown in the early 1950s; partly because his father, who was a clergyman, had a calling with itinerant responsibilities. Ministerial work required movement from place to place in Freetown and the provinces of Sierra Leone.[1] During the late 1950s, he attended the WAM Collegiate School, which was situated at Circular Road. He was also among the cohort of students who moved over to Wilkinson Road from Circular Road. Not long after the transfer, he left to attend the Magburaka Secondary School where his elder brother was a principal.

After completing his secondary school education, he worked for the Customs Department before proceeding to Fourah Bay College (FBC) for undergraduate education. In 1971, he graduated from FBC with a bachelor of arts and a Diploma in Education and went to teach at St. Helena Secondary School. Rev. Smith was made Senior Tutor and Head of the Afternoon Shift at St. Helena after eventful years of service at the school. He remained

---

1. Interview (1985) with Rev. Z. S. F. Smith.

a Senior Teacher at the school till 1980 when he was elected to be principal of the Collegiate School.

Principal Smith arrived at the school when physical and emotional damages had to be repaired. The students had just staged a rebellion, chairs were insufficient, the Board had been appalled by compromising decisions, and the structural plans for rehabilitation were in suspension. The entire school campus was unsecured and the school had been plagued by theft.

The perimeter fence that was intended to secure the school's campus since the 1960s was broken at several points and neighboring residents used the school's property to dump refuse because of the accessibility of the campus.[2] The ground floor of the main building, the staffroom, secretary's office, and the principal's office were all unsecured. Thieves had removed glass louvres from windows in order to steal from offices and buildings.[3] The assembly hall was not spared from the vandalism that had overtaken the school. The financial resources of the school were equally inadequate to meet the infrastructural challenges at hand.

The main building of the school (the classroom block) was without electricity because the school was indebted to the Electricity Corporation (as it was called then) to the tune of one thousand and forty-five leones, and sixty-three cents (Le 1,045.63).[4] All the taps in the science laboratory were out of order and dysfunctional. The roofs of the classroom buildings had serious cracks and the physical state of the school was ocularly deplorable. At the time, the buildings had been constructed about two decades ago.

The school was also indebted to various companies; for example, the school owed the Guma Valley Water Company four thousand and fifty-one leones, and thirty-three cents (Le 4,051.33); the Post and Telecommunications three hundred and five leones (Le 305); and the Republic of Sierra Leone Military Forces (RSLMF) one thousand and eight leones (Le 1,008).[5] Congestion compounded the financial and structural problems of the school by the start of the 1980/81 academic year.

---

2. The Collegiate School Report (1980/1) 2–3.
3. The Collegiate School Report (1980/1) 2–3.
4. The Collegiate School Report (1980/1) 2–3.
5. Minutes of the Collegiate School PTA, First Terminal Meeting, October 3, 1980.

The Administration of Rev. Cannon Z. S. F. Smith (1980-98)

6.1 The Administration of the Rev. Smith (1980-98)

Principal Smith recognized the problems confronting the school and immediately utilized the PTA to assist in solving the problems. The role of the PTA, as conceptualized by Mr. Moiba, became very consequential. The British experiment held great promise for the school. In 1980, officials of the PTA included Mr. J. R. Thorpe (President), Mrs. M. Williams (Secretary), Mrs. Scotland (Treasurer), and Mr. J. D. Cowan (Social Secretary). At the time, the offices of the president and the secretary had not changed since 1975.

Mr. J. R. Thorpe (1916-2012)
Retired Inspector of Prisons & President PTA (1975-ca. 1987)

The PTA was willing to contribute to the success of the new administration by providing financial and moral support. Since its existence in the 1970s, the organization had a history of cooperation with administrators of the school. Apart from the multiple financial contributions to the school by the organizations in bygone years, the organization spent two thousand leones (Le 2,000) to purchase chairs during the 1979/80 academic year. It helped the new administration to defray the cost of arrears for electricity supply by donating one thousand leones (Le 1000).[6]

6. Minutes of the Collegiate School PTA, First Terminal Meeting, October 3, 1980

The principal lobbied the Ministry of Education for some furniture to redress the problem of the scarce supply of chairs and desks. In 1980, the Ministry of Education was able to provide 400 chairs and 250 desks. Further assistance was provided by the Ministry through hire purchase (installment payments) to the tune of one thousand and eight leones (Le 1,008).[7] These amounts, which are seemingly or perceptibly very paltry—because of today's inflationary situation—were very substantial and significant disbursements and arrangements at the time when they were provided or granted.

The contributions of the PTA and the Ministry of Education made it possible for the school to have adequate seating accommodations during the formative years of the Smith administration. The change of circumstances made it possible for the principal to increase enrollment during the 1982/83 and 1983/84 academic years. The proprietors provided an additional ten thousand four hundred and eight leones (Le 10,408) towards the development of the school.[8]

Before the transition to the 1982 accommodations, congestion was clearly a problem. Undisciplined students with poorer academic records had been admitted from other secondary schools. Though the Collegiate School provided an avenue for second chances, some students did not avail themselves of the opportunity to reorient their academic prospects. They continued to be marred by bad behaviors and ill motivations. Poorly behaved students provided auspicious opportunities to reduce the congestion at the school. Some students were dismissed or expelled to stabilize the student population and bring it in conformity with the seating capacity. Hence, by the end of the first year of his tenure, Principal Smith dismissed 186 students.[9] Reduction in the student population coincided with some structural revitalization.

The decrepit fifth Form building was renovated, a stage was constructed for special occasions like prize-giving ceremonies, the entire classroom block was painted and its leaky roof repaired. Renovation work was extended to include the library. The library operated at suboptimal capacity in the previous two years prior to the 1980/1 academic year with some structural damages. Some of the window panes of the library were broken or missing and the seating accommodation was inadequate and uncomfortable. The

---

7. Minutes of the Collegiate School PTA, First Terminal Meeting, October 3, 1980; see also the Collegiate School Report for the 1980/81 academic year.

8. The Collegiate School Report (1980/1) 1.

9. Interview (1985) with Rev. Z. S. F. Smith.

cupboards in the library clumsily held damaged locks and the library was not suitable for quiet reading.

With damaged locks and windows, it was very understandable why some of the books in the library were missing or could not be accounted for. It is both dismaying and pitiful to observe that some students were mostly responsible for the deplorable state of affairs in the school. For a start, the principal addressed the window and ventilation problems of the library. The elegant British-styled glass louvres that had formerly adorned the modernized campus at Wilkinson Road were replaced by ventilation blocks that could not be vandalized at exorbitant replacement costs.

Newer cupboards were brought in to protect the remnants of costly volumes of books and new locks were installed.[10] Chairs became available for the library and students and faculty members were able to comfortably utilize the library. The principal considered the library to be an integral part of the school:

> A school worthy of its name ought to boast of a good library. For if the pupils fail to acquire the ability to engage in purposeful research at this stage in their career the school will be failing in its primary role of moulding its pupils for the future.[11]

The revitalization of the library also included the acquisition of valuable books. In June 1981, the school acquired textbooks for various subjects to the tune of one thousand six hundred and twenty leones (Le 1,620) from Forster Plan International; thereby providing additional resources for students and faculty.[12] The library was developed to have reference and circulatory components in the 1980s and library reading was integrated in the school's curriculum.[13] Increased academic resources naturally complemented increased academic standards, responsibilities, and performances.

By focusing on academic resources, the Smith administration also demanded higher academic productivity from the Collegiate students. Ever since the 1960s, the threshold for promotion was set at a lower bar of an aggregate or cumulative performance of 45 percent. The lower threshold

10. The Collegiate School Report (1980/1) 7.

11. Rev. Z. S. F. Smith in The Collegiate School Report (1980/1).

12. The Collegiate School Report (March 1981–February 1982) 5; see also June 16, 1981, broadcasting news about the Collegiate School, compiled by the Ministry of Information.

13. See Broadcasting News about the Collegiate School, compiled by the Ministry of Information, June 16, 1981.

The West African Methodist Collegiate School, 1911–2021

was increased to 50 percent for the 1982/83 academic year and beyond. Additionally, students were required to perform reasonably well in mathematics and english in order to be promoted. Promotion to Form 5 required satisfactory performance in at least six courses.[14] The changes generated ocular academic successes. The students had been given opportunities to succeed and were challenged to elevate their academic performance; they did just that in 1984 with a 96 percent rate of success in public examination (see Figure 6.1). The list of teachers who contributed to the successes in the 1980s (excluding those who joined in 1985) can be found in Table 6.1.

The Smith administration also revitalized agriculture. Agriculture was a recurrent and historic aspect of academic life since the formation of the Old Collegiate School though its fortune waxed and waned. Nevertheless, it became an integral part of the school's curriculum in the 1980s.[15] The basic ambition of the principal was to reduce the overconcentration on much more traditional courses in the classroom so that students can expand their orientation of learning to engage in practical things. We may recall that Professor Faduma introduced agriculture to the school's curriculum in 1917. Agriculture was not given serious consideration as part of the school's curriculum since the resuscitation of the school in 1948.

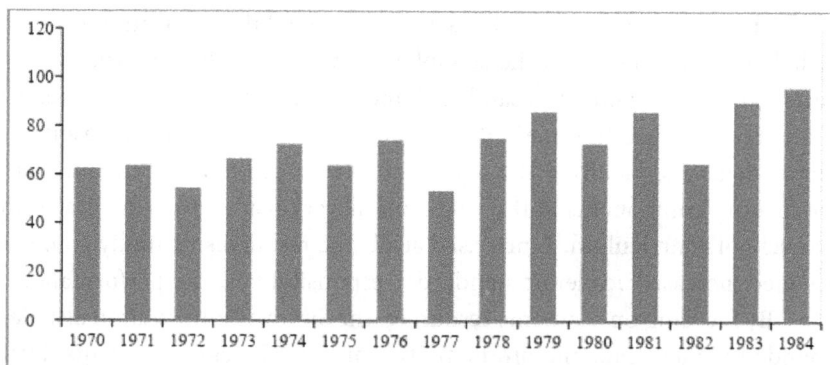

Figure 6.1: Certificate/GCE O'Level Results (Percentage of Success, 1970–84)

---

14. The Collegiate School Report (1983/84) 3; see also the Collegiate School Report (March 1980–February 1981) 3.

15. The Collegiate School Report (1983/84) 5.

The Administration of Rev. Cannon Z. S. F. Smith (1980-98)

Table 6.1: Faculty Members 1984/5 and 1985

Name/Qualification	Name/Qualification	Name/Qualification
Rev. Z. S. F Smith, BA, DipEd	Mr. K. Macauley, BA, DipEd	Mr. K. E. Turay, BA, MEd
Mrs. M. P. Decker, BA (Hons), TAC	Mr. O. Dixon, HTC	Mrs. E. Leigh, BA.
Mrs. M. Davies, BSc, TAC	Miss. M. Webber, HTC	Mrs. J. Leigh, BA.
Mrs. H. Kawaley, BA, DipEd	Mr. L. A. B. Macauley, TC	Miss. D. Patewa, BA, DipEd
Mr. S. B. Moiba, BA, DipEd	Miss. C. E. E. Buckle, HTC, TC	Mrs. V. Carlton-Carew, HTC
Mrs. O. Jackson, BA, DipEd	Mr. C. V. C. Macrae, HTC	Mrs. A. M. Banya, BEd
Mrs. I. Dougan, BA, DipEd	Miss. J. Johnson, HTC.	Mr. A. Adams, BA.
Miss. A. Fillie-Faboe, BEd	Mr. S. D. O. Faux, HTC.	Mr. J. Tengbeh, BEng (Hons.)
Mr. I. J. A. Solomon (Solo), HTC.	Mr. C. Bell, BEng (Hons.)	1985 and After*
Mrs. J. B. O. Harding, BSc, DipEd	Mr. A. Uyimadu, BSc	*Mrs. V. Perry, BEd, MEd*
Mr. C. M. C. Sesay, BSc, DipEd	Mrs. B. M. Jones, HTC	*Mr. L. E. T. Taylor, BA, DipEd*
Miss. D. Nicol-Wilson, BSc (Hons.)	Miss. P. John, HTC	*Miss. N. A. K. Taylor, HTC*
Mr. E. M. Davies, BEng (Hons.).	Mr. V. L. A. Venn, "A" Levels	*Miss. G. Hamilton, BA (Hons.), DipEd*
Miss. E. Wyndham, BSc, DipEd	Miss. E. John, HTC.	*Mr. Lightfoot-Taylor, HTC.*
Mrs. C. Jenkins-Johnston, BA, DipEd	Miss. J. Kargbo, BA (Hons.), DipEd	*Mr. C. E. S. Warburton, BA (Hons.)*

* *List of members in 1985 is not exhaustive. Miss N. A. K. Taylor (now Mrs. Warburton) and Miss. G. Hamilton (now Mrs. Lightfoot-Taylor).* Administrative Staff: *Mrs. M.*

The West African Methodist Collegiate School, 1911-2021

Richards (Secretary), Mr. L. J. Y. Coker (Cokie) (Bursar) and Miss F. R. A. George (Clerk/Typist); Laboratory Assistants: *Mr. H. Sankoh, Mr. P. Campbell, and Mr. S. Kanu.*

The reintroduction of Agriculture into the school's curriculum caught the attention and interest of students.[16] Agricultural science made progress under the tutelage of Mr. Ola Dixon, who became the agricultural science teacher after the reintroduction of the subject matter into the school's curriculum in the 1983/4 academic year. The subject matter was introduced to be part of the curriculum of Form 1 students (for junior students) but in 1985 Agricultural Science was offered to Form 2 students.

One of the most longlasting achievements of the Smith administration was the creation of the school's marching band. Efforts had been made since the 1960s to create a marching band to no avail. The school suffered embarrassment in the 1970s when no marching band showed up to grace it's thanksgiving celebration. Marching bands of the schools in Freetown had a propensity to turn up late or not show up at all. Unspectacular contingencies were no longer tolerable options for the alumni association and the principal. Therefore, the principal mobilized all the necessary resources to create a functional marching band for the Collegiate School.

After collecting all the essential equipments, six instructors were put in charge of the marching band and the instructors started practice sessions. At the start, practices were conducted daily and the principal had to stay in school till 6 PM on several occasions.[17] Practice sessions were subsequently reduced to three days a week as the students became more proficient and comfortable with the instruments. The principal designed the uniform for the marching band and got the alumni association to assist with purchasing the materials for the uniform, which was predominantly made up of the school's colors of yellow and purple.[18] The improbable dream of having a uniquely Collegiate School marching band eventually materialized.

On February 1, 1983, the marching band of the school was inaugurated and formally launched by an alumnus and Chairman of the BoGs, Hon. Major General J. S. Momoh (later President of the Republic of Sierra Leone). The Chairman of the Board was a major patron in the effort to bring the marching band to fruition. He was one of those who helped to purchase the instruments when Mr. Ralph Wright was the band instructor.

16. The Collegiate School Report 1983/84, 5.
17. Interview (1985) with Rev. Z. S. F. Smith.
18 Interview (1985) with Rev. Z. S. F. Smith.

The Administration of Rev. Cannon Z. S. F. Smith (1980-98)

Mr. J. R. Thorpe, President of the PTA, chaired the occasion and the Rev. J. A. D. Davies, General Superintendent of the WAM church, dedicated the instruments to God in the tradition of the Christian faith.

Major General Momoh observed that the day was a "red-letter-day" in the annals of the school's history. He recapitulated the conceptualization of the marching band by Mr. I. T. A. Wallace Johnson.[19] The day's occasion, he observed, was a fulfillment of the aims and aspirations for which Mr. I. T. A. Wallace-Johnson strove "ceaselessly and assiduously"[20] The ceremony ended with a vote of thanks by Mr. S. B. Moiba, a faculty member.

The marching band started with about thirty members: ten of the members were percussion players; six were trombone players; three were saxophone players; two were clarinet players; two were "E" flat bass players, and a drum major.[21] The school's marching band performed for the very first time in February 1983, on the occasion of the school's thanksgiving service. Hundreds of people cheered the bandsmen and the principal, as the principal marched to the music of what had been a very improbable marching band. It was a joyous occasion and a moment of pride for the alumni association and the principal to have their own marching band put up a spectacular and memorable performance.

Photo by IMS Vintage Photos
President J. S. Momoh, OBE, Alumnus of the WAM Collegiate School

19. *The Collegiate Grapevine*, no.8 (May 1984) 7.
20. *The Collegiate Grapevine*, no.8 (May 1984) 7.
21. *The Collegiate Grapevine*, no.8 (May 1984) 29.

Indeed, it was a great day for the school. No longer could the school be publicly disappointed and embarrassed because of the failure of others to show up in moments of public need. At the time of this writing (2020), the marching band continues to spectacularly perform on the streets of Freetown. After a brief period of existence, the marching band was able to impressively compete at the national level. In December 1984, the band won first place in an inter-schools competition held in the Bintumani Hotel. It subsequently went on to earn impressive successes by competing at very high levels.

The school continued to regularly observe annual events and extra-curricular activities such as prize-giving ceremonies, Foundation Day celebrations, L&DS meetings, and scouting activities. Under the leadership of Mr. Campbell, the 16th Freetown Scout Troop was restructured to have six patrols: Tiger, Wolf, Fox, Lion, Bull, and Owl.[22] A Court of Honour was responsible for the administrative welfare of the troop. The court consisted of the Troop Leader, the Patrol Leaders, and the Assistant Patrol Leaders.[23] Scouts generally have an internal process of discipline.

Discipline was maintained as a consistent policy of the school. The first principal emphasized its moral imperative and linked academic discipline at the secondary level with that of the tertiary. Classes started very early in the morning so that students can be acquainted with waking up very early in the morning for official business. Professor Faduma punished junior students for idling around with senior students. Principal Hastings-Spaine assumed responsibility for student behavior within the confines of the school. Principal Rogers-Wright gave chase to students for bad behavior beyond the perimeter of the school.

Principal Smith adopted the model of Principal Rogers-Wright and played a role for the discipline of students beyond the frontiers of the campus. This style of discipline did not foreclose the responsibility of parents and guardians to ensure the good behavior of students out of the classroom. Discipline was seen as a collaborative endeavor of the administration and parents or guardians. Punctuality was emphasized and truancy was severely punished. At the start of the 1984/5 academic year, five students were suspended for leaving the school before the end of the school day.[24] Student truancy was reduced by severe penalties, which acted as a deterrent.

22. *The Collegiate Grapevine*, no.7 (May 1982) 61.
23. *The Collegiate Grapevine*, no.8 (May 1984) 63.
24. Interview (1985) with Ms. Muriel Webber, Secretary PTA.

The Administration of Rev. Cannon Z. S. F. Smith (1980-98)

The renovation of the fence also helped to minimize truancy during the Smith administration. Students will periodically damage the fence at obscure and virtually undetectable locations to increase the prospects of truancy. It required diligent inspection and determination to repair the loopholes in the security system of the school. Apparently, over time, student discipline woefully deteriorated and became a pale shadow of what was envisaged in the formative years of the school. The repair work maximized the difficulties of breaching the campus perimeter. The principal stayed on top of discipline for good reasons. He was convinced that the school will always:

> endorse the right values and inculcate in the pupils those qualities which will make them responsible citizens[25] ... even at the expense of being termed hard, the school which aims at succeeding must set high standards, first in behavior and high standards in all other spheres of school life will be obtained.[26]

Institutional regulations cannot be conceived in their imagination.[27] The principal was subsequently nicknamed, "*Discipline*," by the students.

The Rev. Smith continued the policy of gender diversification and the recruitment of qualified faculty members. For the first time in the history of the school, a coeducational system was established for senior students who were interested in business and professional studies. There were thirty-one full time faculty members in the 1980/81 academic year, twenty-five of whom were university graduates; three were holders of HTC and two had Advanced Teacher's Certificates.[28] From March 1981 to February 1982, some faculty members left to be employed elsewhere. Ten teachers were employed to teach and replace the departed teachers. Mrs. M. Davies, who was on study leave, reunited with the faculty. Six of the newly employed were degree holders; two of the remaining faculty members had HTC and one had "O" Level Certificate.[29] The principal hired two part-time teachers, Mr. E. T. Nelson-Williams (mathematics) and Miss. D. Nicol-Wilson (economics), in order to augment the shortfall of available faculty members. The teachers were employed to teach mathematics and economics at the fourth and fifth Form levels.

---

25. The Collegiate School Report (March 1980–February 1981) 7.
26. The Collegiate School Report (March 1981–February 1982) 7.
27. The Collegiate School Report (March 1981–February 1982) 7.
28. The Collegiate School Report (1980/81) 5.
29. The Collegiate School Report (March 1981–February 1982) 3-4.

The West African Methodist Collegiate School, 1911–2021

Departures and arrivals continued in the 1982/83 academic year. Six teachers left the school and eleven were added to the faculty. Five of those who were added had university degrees, four were HTC holders, one had a Teaching Certificate, and the other had an Occupational Certificate in Business Studies (OCBS).[30] In the 1983/84 academic year, eleven faculty members joined the staff to replace eight teachers. Five of those who joined were degree holders, five had HTC and one had an "A" Level Certificate.[31] The academic successes of the students in the 1980s (see Figure 6.1) must have been positively correlated to the quality of the faculty; 1984/5 was particularly impressive.

For the year ending in July 1981, the school entered eighty-six candidates for the SC/GCE Exams; twelve students outrightly failed the exams. This was, however, an incremental improvement on the performance of the students in the 1979/80 examinations, which registered a 72 percent rate of success. The 1981/82 data are distortionary because of widespread (national) academic irregularities. Ten subjects were cancelled, which makes the data rather noisy and insufficient to characterize the performance of the Collegiate students. The cancelled subjects included English language and literature, history, mathematics, chemistry, agricultural science, economics, and biology.

Innocent students were harshly punished because of the agglomeration effects—the inability to distinguish beneficiaries of fraud from the innocents. There was no failure in the French exam; the three students who attempted the exam successfully passed the exam. In physics, four students passed the exam; seven students failed. As a result of the irregularities in the 1981/82 exams, a lot of students had to attempt the exams in the 1982/83 academic year. The school entered seventy-seven students. Virtually all of the students (about twenty) who attempted the exams in 1981/82 had to retake the exam in 1982/3 because of the previous year's cancellations; fourteen of the seventy-seven students gained Division 3 passes, fifty-six gained GCE "O" Level passes, two were absent, and five outrightly failed the exams, implying a 90 percent rate of success.

In the following year (1983/4), seventy-one students attempted the exams; four gained Division 2 passes, eighteen gained School Certificate Division 3 passes, forty-six gained GCE "O" Level passes, and three outrightly failed the exams. For the first time, one of the students was able to

30. The Collegiate School Report (1982/83) 2.
31. The Collegiate School Report (1983/84) 4.

The Administration of Rev. Cannon Z. S. F. Smith (1980-98)

get a distinction in history after the 1978 performance in history (a record that the author proudly guarded for many years). The school continued to expand its structural changes.

At the suggestion of Mrs. K. E. Turay, BA, MEd, a self-help building project was initiated.[32] The proposed project was set up to raise funds for a wood workshop, conference hall, and teaching and communal accommodation. After displaying the preliminary architectural plans and costs, it was decided that an ad hoc committee should be established to expedite the construction of the buildings. On June 13, 1983, a Self-Help Building Committee was created, consisting of faculty members. Members of the committee included Mrs. Miranda Decker, vice principal and Chair Lady of the Committee; Mrs. K. E. Turay (Secretary); Mrs. Hannah Kawaley;[33] Mrs. Georgiana Tucker; Mrs. Mary Davies (one of my math teachers); Mrs. O. Jackson (one of my English literature teachers), Mrs. I. Dougan, Mr. C. Sesay, Mr. S. B. Moiba, Mr. Ernest Cummings, Mr. G. Gbongbor, and Mr. R. P. A. Sawyerr.

The project was formally launched on November 1, 1983, under the Chairmanship of Major General J. S. Momoh. Prominent individuals witnessed the occasion, including Hon. Shamsu Mustapha (who deputized the Hon. Siaka Kanu), Parliamentary Special Assistant, Ministry of Economic and Development Planning; Rev. Z. F. S. Smith (principal); Rev. J. A. D. Davies (the General Superintendent of the WAM church); and Mr. Moses Koroma of the Ministry of Education.

On June 24, 1983 the committee members decided to have two fundraising events—a sponsored walk and moonlight picnic. Their efforts proved to be fruitful. The sponsored walk, which was made from the school's campus to Aberdeen Village on November 5, 1983, generated about five thousand leones (Le 5,000). The moonlight picnic on December 3, 1983, generated three thousand eight hundred and forty-eight leones (Le 3,848). By 1985, the Committee was able to generate fourteen thousand leones (Le 14,000) from the donations and proceeds of the sponsored walk and moonlight picnic. One of the endeavors, which totaled over three million leones, proved to be overambitious and out of reach.

Just before the outbreak of all-out civil war in 1991, some national educational policies were mandated by the national government. In the early 1990s, the educational system of the country was in crisis. The crisis

---

32. *The Collegiate Grapevine*, no.8 (May 1984) 31

33. Also one of the author's English literature teachers. Students nicknamed her "*Miss Havisham*," one of the characters in Charles Dickens' *Great Expectations*.

was induced by a multiplicity of factors, which Alghali and others identify as, among other things, poor financial support, inappropriate curricula, the start and intensification of the rebel (civil) war, and a dim view of the value of education by the youths.[34]

The decline in enrollment at the primary and secondary levels and virtual stagnation at the tertiary level discouraged the pursuit of education. Between 1968 and 1992, students protested against the apathetic predisposition of policy makers to establish sounder foundations for educational advancement and economic opportunities.

Social discontents created fertile opportunities for the usurpation of civilian regimes and during the war, a military coup, under the leadership of Captain Valentine Strasser, deposed the civilian government of President Joseph Saidu Momoh (an alumnus) and established a National Provisional Ruling Council (NPRC) on April 29, 1992. The junta ruled till 1996, two years shy of the retirement of Principal Smith. The military regime modified the national educational system. A new system, "the 6-3-3-4," was introduced to the country in 1993, which was also issued in the New Education Policy of 1995 (see Table 6.2). A Basic Education Decree was pronounced in 1994 together with a National Education Plan (1994).

The restructured system of education incorporated an ambitious free education component for six years of primary school education. Shortages of facilities, educators, and the destructive aftermath of wars made the application and results of the policy rather challenging if not unrealistic. Students entered junior secondary school and were expected to stay there for three years. For the next three years in senior secondary school, students had a choice (track) of continuing their education to university or pursuing vocational education after junior secondary school to get some practical skills.[35] The civil war disrupted the implementation of the system.

---

34. Alghali et al., "Education in Sierra Leone, 2; see also Jackson, "Proposal for Virtual ICT Use."

35. "Efforts directed towards vocational training focus on reintegrating combatants. Given that 2/3 of the adult population is involved in subsistence agriculture, the main thrusts are agricultural skills, and related proficiencies such as mechanics, carpentry and bricklaying . . .

There are only two universities in Sierra Leone, namely Njala University (established as an Agricultural Experimentation Station in 1910), and the University of Sierra Leone, founded as Fourah Bay College in 1827. The former has colleges of education, community health services, social sciences, agriculture, environmental sciences, and technology, while the latter has dedicated itself to excellence in teaching, learning, and community service, through a wider range of programs;" see https://www.scholaro.com/

The Administration of Rev. Cannon Z. S. F. Smith (1980–98)

Table 6.2: The 6-3-3-4 System of Education in Sierra Leone

Education	School/Level	Grades	Age	Years
Primary	Primary	1–6	6–12	6
Middle	Junior Secondary	1–3	12–15	3
Secondary	Secondary	1–3	15–18	3
Vocational	Vocational education			
Tertiary	Bachelor			4
Tertiary	Master			1–2
Tertiary	Doctorate			3

Source: Scholaro Pro

At the end of six years of primary education, students took the National Primary School Examination (NPSE). Successful students then proceeded to junior secondary school for junior secondary education, which was expected to last for three years. The students then took the Basic Education Certificate Examination (BECE), which gave them a ticket to senior secondary school if they were successful. At the end of senior secondary school, the senior students were expected to take the West African Secondary School Certificate Examination (WASSCE), the equivalent of the SC/GCE. Students who satisfied the requirements for undergraduate work could then proceed to university for a four-year-degree course. Of course, vocational training was also an option.

Civil war started as the educational system was being restructured. The precise date of the commencement of war in the provinces of Sierra Leone can be controversial but the year, 1991, is irrefutable. As the war eventually engulfed Freetown, the tenure of Principal Smith came to an end in 1998. The next and final chapter takes a look at the consequences of the war and pandemics on education in general and the Collegiate School in particular.

---

pro/Countries/Sierra-Leone/Education-System.

7

The Consequences of War and Pandemics (1991–2021)

AFTER SEVERAL YEARS OF sporadic student protests and relative calm, Sierra Leone was plunged into an all-out civil war in 1991. The war prefaced two pandemics, Ebola and COVID-19; one of which (Ebola) devastated the country and the educational prospects of students. In explicit terms, the continuity of education was disrupted with adverse externalities. National electronic programs tentatively replaced the traditional delivery of educational materials.

7.1 Civil War in Sierra Leone (1991–2002)

The date of commencement of the war is imprecise but it is officially believed that the war started on March 23, 1991. The official date is associated with attempts to pointedly overthrow the government of President Joseph Saidu Momoh, an alumnus of the WAM Collegiate School. The Revolutionary United Front (RUF) under Foday Sankoh, with support of Liberian rebel leader, Charles Taylor, and his group, the National Patriotic Front of Liberia (NFPL), spearheaded the assault of what became one of the bloodiest civil wars in Africa. The war claimed the lives of more than 50,000 people and displaced thousands. If the *casus belli* is imprecise and rather amorphous, the conditions for the prolongation of war were more precise. At the center of the ruthless war was a fight of the violent

The Consequences of War and Pandemics (1991-2021)

extraction of diamonds for inordinate wealth and control of political power to ensure control over the diamond fields.

Actually, the war emerged out of deep-seated animosity between the leaders of Sierra Leone and Liberia. By 1990, the state structure in Liberia had collapsed and the military wing of the Economic Community of West African States (ECOWAS), Economic Community of West African States Monitoring Group (ECOMOG), had used Sierra Leone as a base (launching pad) for successful operations in Liberia.[1] The operations were successful but they also enraged the Liberian rebel leader, Charles Taylor, who was prevented by ECOMOG from capturing the capital city of Liberian, Monrovia.

Taylor acrimoniously targeted Sierra Leone, a villainous country with very lucrative diamond fields that could easily pay for the cost of recruiting and retaining mercenary soldiers. The RUF was aided by a very capable accomplice, Charles Taylor, who was also interested in beneficial retaliatory outcomes. Accordingly, the coalition of RUF and Taylor's National Patriotic Front (NPF) coalesced around a common hatred of the APC regime.[2] During the first year of the war, the RUF took control of the diamond-rich territories in eastern and southern areas of Sierra Leone, encouraged by a naïve presumption that the war would not reach the capital city, Freetown.

The RUF launched its first campaign into eastern Kailahun (the eastern Province of Sierra Leone) in March 1991 with Sankoh at the head of his soldiers and some Burkinabe mercenaries. The war ultimately got to Freetown in 1999. The ferocity, longevity, and barbarism of the war caught international attention as the war progressed to Freetown. In March 1993, ECOMOG sent troops, predominantly made up of Nigerians, to Freetown in order to assist the Sierra Leone Army (SLA) in recapturing the diamond districts.

A secondary objective was to push the RUF to the Sierra Leone-Liberia border. By the end of 1993, many observers thought the war had ended because the RUF ceased most of its military operations; the RUF soldiers merely dispersed. Great Britain, Guinea, and the United States joined the ECOMOG forces to fight the RUF and its mercenaries from Liberia (Charles Taylor's NPFL), Libya, and Burkina Faso. Shifting alliances, chicanery, double-dealing, and competing international interests made it impossible to successfully prosecute the war to completion in a

---

1. Warburton, *Evolution of Crises*, 79–84.

2. Some students in high schools and Fourah Bay College had misgivings about the APC regime—under the leadership of Siaka Stevens—and had launched violent demonstrations in Freetown during the 1970s and 1980s. Some students were imprisoned or expelled and some lecturers were fired.

timely manner; panic started to take hold in Freetown as the specter of expansion became real.

On April 29, 1992, a military coup led by Captain Valentine Strasser ousted President Joseph Momoh. Captain Strasser's National Provisional Ruling Council (NPRC) asserted that the ousted government was corrupt and incapable of revitalizing the national economy to repel the existential threat confronting the country. The war evolved and metastasized into brutality beyond imagination as the civilian population was traumatized; many were amputated, decapitated, or hacked to death. Evidently, the savagery was a far cry from benign ideas that had been ostensibly proposed to liberate the civilian population from political oppression and economic deprivation.[3] Homes of the civilian population were looted, females raped, and children recruited to fight as "child soldiers" and mine diamonds that were sold at 10 percent less than their market value.[4]

While civilians were being attacked and mutilated, the warring factions did not necessarily exchange fire in the theaters of war (Matsumoto). Both the SLA soldiers (and ex-soldiers) and the RUF occasionally disguised themselves to create images of their opponents. As a result, a term, *sobels*, or "soldiers by day, rebels by night" was used to characterize the ad hoc composition of fighters.[5]

On March 29, 1995, the Sierra Leone Government retained a South Africa-based mercenary group, Executive Outcomes (EO), to finally defeat the RUF. The retreating RUF signed the Abidjan Peace Accord, which purportedly brought an end to the fighting. Sierra Leone installed an elected civilian government (Ahmad Tejan Kabbah) in March 1996. However, hostilities continued! On May 25, 1997, another group of Sierra Leone Army officers staged another coup and established the Armed Forces Revolutionary Council (AFRC) as the new government of the country.

The officers invited the RUF to join them with little resistance or upheaval in Freetown.[6] The collusion between the supposed rivals (archenemies) of the RUF and SLA became more apparent in May 1997 when an SLA officer, Johnny Paul Koroma, executed a successful coup against

---

3. The original objective of the RUF was to overthrow the All Peoples' Congress (APC), the political party of President Momoh, in order to create a more egalitarian society by colluding with some soldiers of the Sierra Leonean Armed Forces (SLA).

4. Campbell, *Blood Diamonds*, 43.

5. Keen, *Conflict and Collusion*.

6. Momodu, "Sierra Leone Civil War (1991–2002)," para. 4.

The Consequences of War and Pandemics (1991–2021)

the democratically elected government of President Kabbah; the RUF was invited to be part of the Armed Forces Revolutionary Council (AFRC).

The new government under Johnny Paul Koroma declared the end of hostilities.

Notwithstanding, looting, rape, and murder, mostly by RUF forces, promptly ensued after the pronouncement of an end of hostilities. The disturbances evinced an obvious lack of control over the affairs of the country for which the ECOMOG forces had to return to recapture Freetown. Ahmad Tejan Kabbah took office again on February 13, 1998. Hostilities continued in the country with an unequivocal clarity that the civil war was far from over.

World leaders brokered negotiations between the RUF and the Sierra Leone Government in January 1999. The Lomé Peace Accord was signed on July 7, 1999. RUF Commander, Foday Sankoh, was made vice president and granted control over Sierra Leone's diamond mines in return for a cessation of hostilities and the deployment of a UN peacekeeping force to monitor the disarmament process. However, with intermittent hostilities and rebel advancement to Freetown in May 2000, RUF was noncompliant. With the help of the United Nations forces, British troops, and Guinean air support, the Sierra Leone Army finally defeated the RUF before another siege and control of Freetown. On January 18, 2002, newly installed President Ahmad Tejan Kabbah declared the Sierra Leone Civil War had finally ended.[7] On July 28, 2002, the British withdrew a 200-strong military contingent that had been in Sierra Leone since the summer of 2000, leaving behind a training team of about 140 military personnel to train and professionalize the SLA and Navy.

The consequences of the war were both pervasive and horrific. It is estimated that probably close to 75,000 were killed, 20,000 were mutilated,[8] two million were displaced, and tens of thousands of women and girls were raped or forced into sex slavery.[9] Hundreds of schools were destroyed. The United Nations International Children's Emergency Fund (UNICEF) estimated that 1,270 primary schools were destroyed and that about 67 percent of all school-aged children were out of school in the year 2001.[10]

---

7. Momodu, "Sierra Leone Civil War (1991–2002)," para. 6.

8. Hoffman, "Civilian Target in Sierra Leone," 216.

9. Dougherty, "Searching for Answers," 39; Matsumoto, "Young People, Education," 107.

10. Ozisik, "Education in Sierra Leone," para. 1.

The West African Methodist Collegiate School, 1911–2021

Obviously, the Collegiate School was not insulated from the turbulence and destruction. The educational system of any country is systemic and significant disruptions in any part of the system will have systemic consequences. When primary schools are decimated, secondary schools will be starved. The system of education in Sierra Leone consists of three basic levels with subclassifications: primary, junior secondary, and senior secondary. Students begin junior secondary school around the age of twelve and remain at that level through age fifteen. Schools and colleges were closed down as a result of the war. Secondary school participation, which had been less robust and affirmed by decline in literacy rates, was severely affected by the war. Net attendance ratio declined from 2008 to 2012 by about 39.9 percent for boys and 33.2 percent for girls.[11] War also creates displacements.

Migration creates spatial problems, demand for limited resources, and congestion. Accordingly, for quite some time the Collegiate School had to operate day and evening shifts to accommodate displaced students as a result of the increased student population in Freetown. The temporary closure of schools and colleges as a result of the rebel war also reduced the number of children who actually returned to school. About 60 percent of the children in the age bracket of seven to fourteen years were employed in 2013 because of poverty. The lowest 20 percent of the population had about 8 percent of national wealth in 2018; slightly more than the United States' 5.2 in 2016. Net secondary school enrollment for males was about 43 percent in 2018[12] and the war actually accelerated the pace at which the country lost talents; the ongoing brain-drain syndrome was expedited.

The school had to make readjustments to accommodate population pressures by operating two shifts in the 1990s and about six principals

---

11. At the time of this writing, the Collegiate School is not coeducational. The "boys-only school" does not suffer identical setbacks as co-education or "girls-only" schools. Class completion rate for girls remains very low with high dropout rates and consistently low enrollment in secondary schools. Early pregnancy, gender-based violence, child marriage, and cultural biases propagate the cycle of gender inequality (Ozisik, "Education in Sierra Leone," para. 1).

12. See "Sierra Leone," under the "Education and Literacy" tab, esp. the bottom-most graph from the "Participation in Education" subheader. "Net enrollment rate is the ratio of children of official school age who are enrolled in school to the population of the corresponding official school age. Secondary education completes the provision of basic education that began at the primary level, and aims at laying the foundations for lifelong learning and human development, by offering more subject- or skill-oriented instruction using more specialized teachers" (UNESCO Institute for Statistics).

served during and after the war: Mr. S. E. Beury (1998–99), BA, DipEd, who served as acting principal; Mr. Nathaniel Davies, BA, DipEd, and Mrs. Veronica Perry, BA, MEd (principals after Mr. Beury); Mr. A. Kpakima (2019) and Mr. M. S. T. Koroma (principal for the Senior Secondary School); and Mrs. Miranda Cole (principal for the Junior Secondary School) in 2020. Social and economic disturbances, which started in the late 1980s, generated a brain-drain syndrome with implications for the recruitment and retention of qualified faculty members.

In the 1940s and 1960s, the Collegiate School struggled to recruit and retain qualified teachers. Unfortunately, by the 1990s, a brain-drain syndrome in the country became irreversible as a result of poorer economic conditions, inadequate compensation, and political instability. Most educated Sierra Leoneans have left the country for relatively stable foreign countries with promises of economic prosperity (relatively safer havens). Push factors have resulted in a dearth of qualified teachers (educators).

Though the system of education is a staggered or truncated 6-3-3-4 system, restructuring the system does not translate into the recruitment and retention of qualified teachers. Before the war, and on average, there was a teacher for every nineteen students in the secondary schools of Sierra Leone. The ratio went up to twenty-seven students by the end of the war in 2001.[13] Of course, variations must be expected from school to school. It is noteworthy that the adult literacy rate for those who are fifteen years of age and above is about 43 percent in 2018.[14]

The brain-drain syndrome is positively correlated with the resource-curse syndrome, which had started before the war but was elevated during and after the war. The combination of the two syndromes is also symptomatic of an ailing educational system that affects the Collegiate School in particular and other academic institutions in general. "The fact that countries that are well endowed with resources often do so badly is referred to as the

---

13. Secondary school pupil-teacher ratio is the average number of pupils per teacher in secondary school; see the World Bank's World Development Indicators (2020) at https://databank.worldbank.org/source/world-development-indicators and UNESCO Institute for Statistics.

14. See the World Bank's World Development Indicators (2020) at https://databank.worldbank.org/source/world-development-indicators. UNESCO defines the adult literacy rate is the percentage of people ages fifteen and above who can both read and write with understanding a short simple statement about their everyday life (see "Youth/Adult Literacy Rate," para. 1).

resource curse."[15] There are no easy antidotes for expelling the curse, but privatization, revenue sharing, minimization of corruption and information asymmetry or minimization of illegal diversion of revenue can be good remediating measures for a start.[16] The *resource curse* syndrome has become a conspicuous and common phenomenon in formerly colonized countries with an abundance of national wealth and impoverished citizenry.

Sachs presents an equally compelling proposal for reversing the trajectory of the curse syndrome by appropriately handling and utilizing national wealth.[17] It must be noted that the reference to oil in the resource curse analysis is merely figurative or representative or of the underlying problems in resource-rich African countries. African leaders must quickly learn that it is not too late to focus on public and merit goods to reverse the brain-drain syndrome. Public goods have external effects. They are nonrivalrous and nonexcludable; meaning that someone's consumption of such a good does not preclude others from consuming the good (nonrivalrous). Once a public good or service comes into existence others cannot be excluded from its benefits (nonexcludable). Public goods or services are usually underprovided by the private sector though every society relies on them. They include national defense, adherence to the rule of law, environmental protection, and basic infrastructural networks like roads, power supply, water, and sanitation.[18]

Education falls in the category of a merit service. Merit goods and services should be available for everyone because they engender social harmony (cohesion) and justice. They include basic healthcare, basic education, social insurance for unemployment and disability, adequate basic nutrition, and safe shelter.[19] These goods and services do not arrive on their own accord. They require sincere and diligent long-term planning or budgetary allocations that are facilitated by the appropriate use of natural resources (wealth) rather than waste, fraud, abuse, and misappropriation of national wealth. As such, public investment should be part of a national strategy that complements what the private sector is capable of generating. The glaring

15. Stiglitz and Spiegel, "Series Preface," v.
16. Stiglitz, "What Is the Role of the State?," 23–52.
17. Sachs, "How to Handle the Macroeconomics," 175.
18. Sachs, "How to Handle the Macroeconomics," 175.
19. Sachs, "How to Handle the Macroeconomics," 175.

and serious absence of these national commitments easily results in brain-drain, instability, and war.[20]

Beyond the human toll and disruption of the learning process, the Collegiate School suffered some structural damages that should be expected in cases of belligerence, aggression, or war. Rebel fighters arrogated (commandeered) the property of the school and used the campus as a camping ground. In a curious twist of circumstances, the vicinity at Wilkinson Road became a sphere of hostilities in the 1940s (during the Second World War before the Collegiate School at Wilkinson Road) and the civil war (after the Collegiate School moved to Wilkinson Road). The infrastructure of the school was degraded and reduced to deplorable conditions, necessitating a new phase of reconstruction.

7.2 Pandemics and Education in Sierra Leone

A pandemic is an infectious disease—with probable fatal consequences—that spreads across large regions or continents to adversely affect a large number of people. In recent memory, Sierra Leone has been impacted by two disruptive epidemics—Ebola (May 25, 2014–November 7, 2015)[21] and COVID-19 (April 1, 2020). Pandemics test the healthcare systems of countries and cause widespread havoc that affects the continuity of education. They can also test the infrastructural capacities of countries in extraordinary ways; meaning that countries with better healthcare and infrastructural systems will be able to respond more effectively to pandemics.

Ebola is considered to be a rare but deadly virus that causes fever, body aches, diarrhea, and bleeding (sometimes) inside and outside the body. As the virus spreads through the body, it damages the immune system and organs. It ultimately causes levels of blood-clotting cells to drop, which leads

---

20. It is also noteworthy that appropriate investment decisions have inter-sectoral benefits, whereby the nonresource export sector can also benefit to prevent the "Dutch Disease" syndrome; see also Sachs, "How to Handle the Macroeconomics," 173. The Dutch Disease was first diagnosed as an economic problem after the discovery of natural gas in the Netherlands (1959). There was a shift from the manufacturing sector to gas production, which increased the supply of natural gas and depressed its price to engender adverse terms of trade; especially with the oil shocks of the 1970s. No sector should suffer after the discovery of a resource. Farmers should not shift from agriculture to diamond mining without adequate national guidance to prevent the extermination of agriculture; see also Pugel, *International Economics*, 123–27.

21. The WHO declared Sierra Leone free of Ebola transmission for the first time on 7 November 2015.

The West African Methodist Collegiate School, 1911–2021

to severe and uncontrollable bleeding. The disease was scientifically characterized as Ebola hemorrhagic fever but is now commonly referred to as Ebola virus. Its lethality rate is estimated to be 90 percent. The virus can be transmitted through the interchange of bodily fluids or cross-contaminated contacts with such fluids.

The first confirmed case in Freetown was reported to the WHO on June 23, 2014. Cases in Freetown and the adjacent district of Port Loko initially increased slowly as patients were transferred to Kenema for treatment. However, the disease dispersed rapidly and on August 6, the President declared a national state of emergency. Stringent laws were also passed to punish the concealment of cases. The real surge in cases started in September after the virus gained a foothold in Freetown. Teams were soon struggling to bury as many as thirty bodies per day (WHO).

According to the WHO, by the third week of September, the situation started to stabilize in Kailahun and Kenema but Freetown, Port Loko, Bombali, and Tonkolili districts showed a sharp and alarming spike. Densely populated cities like Freetown faced the gravest dangers because of limited diagnostic and treatment capacities, and difficulties to undertake contact tracing. The increase in density was also a collateral effect of the civil war that had taken place. As many as three families occupied the same household in shifts, which further increased the spread of the disease within families.

By mid-October, there was prevalent transmission of the virus in Freetown and the western districts; more than 400 new suspected cases were being reported each week. All administrative districts nationwide had reported at least one case (WHO). As in Guinea and Liberia, the outbreak in Sierra Leone mushroomed exponentially; especially in Freetown. Freetown consistently accounted for about a third of the cases in the country.[22]

The Collegiate School, like other institutions of learning in Sierra Leone, was closed down in July 2014 only to reopen in April 2015. The righteous fear that the disease would spread in large gatherings, compounded by unsanitary conditions, was palpable even though UNICEF supplied schools with soap, water, and thermometers to check for fever—a significant symptom of the Ebola virus.

---

22. Other areas that experienced intense transmissions were the neighboring districts of Port Loko and Western Rural and, in the eastern part of the country, Kono district on the border with Guinea.

The Consequences of War and Pandemics (1991–2021)

By the end of the Ebola epidemic in Freetown, about five million children (three to seventeen years of age) were out of school.[23] The disease, which killed about 3,800 people, caused a lingering phobia of congregating. Some students stayed away from school after the reopening for fear of infection at school.[24] The deaths of income providers meant that many families were unable to afford food and pay tuition for their children at the same time. As a result, many children had to work to augment the income of their families. Teenage girls were put in a very precarious position. By 2011, the student teacher ratio dropped from 27:1 in 2001 to 21:1 in 2011. While Ebola is a sub-Saharan virus, COVID-19 originated in China and spread to other areas of the world, especially Western Europe, America, and Latin America.

> COVID-19 is the disease caused by a new coronavirus called SARS-CoV-2. WHO first learned of this new virus on 31 December 2019, following a report of a cluster of cases of 'viral pneumonia' in Wuhan, People's Republic of China. COVID-19 affects different people in different ways.[25]

Infected people have reported a wide range of symptoms, from mild symptoms to severe illness.[26]

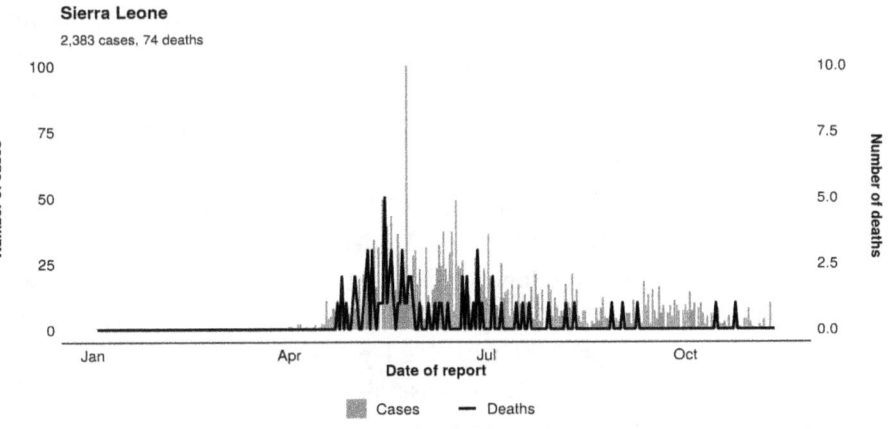

Figure 7.1 COVID-19 Cases and Deaths (April 1, 2020–November 11, 2020)

23. Sifferlin, "5 Million Kids Aren't in School."
24. Fofana, "Sierra Leone Schools Reopen."
25. Cennimo et al., "What Is COVID-19?," para. 1.
26. Additional symptoms include: Fever or chills, fatigue, cough, headache, shortness of breath or difficulty breathing, muscle or body aches, loss of taste or smell, sore throat, congestion or runny nose, nausea or vomiting, and diarrhea.

The West African Methodist Collegiate School, 1911–2021

The first incident of COVID infection was reported on April 1, 2020. In many ways, the government learned a lot from the Ebola pandemic to proactively take measures against the proliferation of the disease in Sierra Leone. The government shut down its airport, realizing that the disease was spreading from China and Western countries. At the time of this writing (November 12, 2020) there have been 2,386 confirmed cases and seventy-four deaths in contrast to the thousands of deaths that had plagued other countries (see Figure 7.1);[27] approximately 1,800 Sierra Leoneans recovered from the disease. The World Bank estimates that the country has an estimated population of 7.65 million (2018).

7.3 Post-Crises Electronic Readjustments of the Educational Infrastructure

In the light of contemporary developments and adversities, the educational infrastructure is no longer what it used to be in 1911. The pandemics, especially COVID, have heightened the importance of technological innovation for the delivery of education when human congregation is unhealthy and infectious. This means that developed and developing countries must now be capable of exploiting technological improvements for the delivery of educational materials in unique or innovative ways.

As the COVID pandemic became rampant in advanced economies, readjustments were made to switch classes from traditional physical contacts to electronic platforms and video conferencing alternatives to avoid the proliferation of an airborne disease. The switch was made to facilitate safer forms of teaching and learning. Evidently, most countries were not prepared for such a revolutionary eventuality. The radical transformation revealed the deficiencies of poverty and/or income inequality when poorer students became incapable of accessing laptops or computers to facilitate their continued education. The disease also revealed the importance of investment in technological innovation and the necessity to have access to the public and merit goods that were discussed earlier; Figure 7.2 is indicative of the necessity.

---

27. Johns Hopkins University data; see https://coronavirus.jhu.edu/map.html.

The Consequences of War and Pandemics (1991-2021)

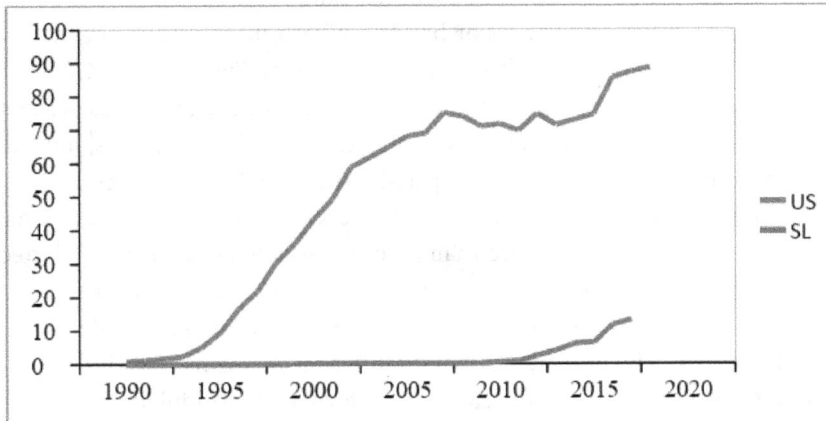

Figure 7.2: Individuals Using the Internet
(Percent of the Population in the United States and Sierra Leone)
Data source: *International Telecommunication Union (ITU), World Telecommunication/ICT Indicators Database, and World Development Indicators (WDI). Internet users are individuals who have used the Internet (from any location) in the last three months. The Internet can be used via a computer, mobile phone, personal digital assistant, gaming console, digital TV, etc.*

The depiction of the percentage of people who have been using the Internet in the United States and Sierra Leone is apparently lopsided. Instinctively, the comparison may seem incongruous and unfair. In reality, it is a very fair comparison that is based on proportion rather than biased absolute values that will favor the richer United States; that is, the illustration shows the percentages of the population of the respective countries that are using the Internet, with the caveat that access and affordability should elicit ancillary considerations.

The percentage of people with access to the Internet in Sierra Leone is relatively miniscule, suggesting that the country needs to be better prepared for pandemics that will ultimately disrupt the delivery of educational materials in the future. Strikingly, the problem of the inequality of access to the Internet in the United States has not been eliminated even with the relatively high percentage of Internet users in the United States. To their credit, the Government of Sierra Leone, in collaboration with the Global Partnership for Education (GPE), cleverly found ways to compensate for the deficiency of Internet users by transmitting educational materials over the airwaves (95.3 FM Education Radio). In so doing, students were also granted an opportunity to get access to educational materials.

The expansion of radio and TV curriculum broadcasting, and the digitalization of learning materials or hands-on "tech literacy" training efforts, also paved the way to train about 85,000 teachers in Sierra Leone. GPE was the main financier to establish and operationalize the Sierra Leone's Teacher Service Commission (TSC), which implemented teacher standards, innovative training, and targets for teaching and institutional performance.

During the Ebola crisis, the best teachers presented educational programs on radio, with more than 80,000 portable radio sets distributed across the country, ensuring that thousands of children continued their learning despite school closures.[28] However, before the pandemic, Sierra Leone heavily relied on traditional learning mechanisms that did not integrate designated electronic learning platforms like Modular Object Oriented Dynamic Learning Environment (MOODLE), Desire2Learn (D2L), and Blackboard.[29] The TSC drew on experience from the Ebola crisis by launching an educational radio program within one week of school closures to continue education during COVID-19 pandemic.

The successful delivery of educational materials by electronic means is contingent on the availability of electricity supply. Unfortunately, Sierra Leone has not invested quality time and resources in the supply of electricity. Relatively wealthier individuals rely on generators to augment the supply of electricity as and when it becomes available. There are obvious undesirable effects that are associated with the inadequacy of electricity or access to electricity. Hospitals and foreign investors rely on the availability and access to energy supply.

Unlike the United States, which has consistently registered one hundred percent access to electricity, the percentage of access to electricity in Sierra Leone is about one-fifth of that figure (see Figure 7.3). Aforesaid, the conceptualization and operationalization (measurement) of access must not be construed as incongruous or biased. It is based on percentages and illustrative of policy (investment) choices rather than wealth disparities that determine affordability. Unfortunately, with enviable resources in Sierra Leone, the country is underperforming. It can perform infinitely better than 26 percent to eliminate the access disparity.

---

28. For further insights, see global partnership, https://www.globalpartnership.org/results/stories-of-change/sierra-leone-power-great-teaching-times-crisis.

29. See also Jackson, "Proposal for Virtual ICT Use."

Table 7.1: Teaching Service Commission: Radio Teaching Program Schedule, October 2020

Time	Sunday	Monday	Tuesday	Wednesday
10:00–11:00		ECD	ECD	ECD
11:00–12:00		English Language 2 (SSS 1–3) Repeat	Chemistry (SSS 1–3) Repeat	Chemistry (SSS 1–3) Repeat
12:00–13:00		Maths (JSS 1–3) Repeat	English Language 1 (SSS 1–3) Repeat	Literature in English 1 (SSS 1–3) Repeat
14:00–15:00		English (Pri) Grades 1–3	Math (Pri) Grades 1–3	Social Studies/Civics (pri) Grades 1–3
15:00–16:00		English (Pri) Grades 4–6	Math (Pri) Grades 4–6	Social Studies/Civics (Pri) Grades 4–6
16:00–17:00		Language Arts1 (JSS 1–3)	Maths (JSS 1–3)	Social Studies/ Civics (JSS 1–3)
17:00–18:00	Music and Meditation	Maths (JSS 1–3)	Integrated Science (JSS 1–3)	Language Arts 1 (JSS 1–3)
18:00–19:00		English Language 1 (SSS 1–3)	Literature in English 1 (SSS 1–3)	Chemistry (SSS 1–3)
19:00–20:00		Maths (SSS 1–3)	English Language 1 (SSS 1–3)	Literature in English 1 (SSS 1–3)
20:00–20:30		Life Skills	Life Skills	Life Skills
20:30–21:30		English Language 1 (SSS) Repeat	Maths (SSS) Repeat	English Language 2 (SSS 1–3) Repeat

Source: MBSSE, Education Broadcasting House

The West African Methodist Collegiate School, 1911–2021

Table 7.1 (contd.) Teaching Service Commission: Radio Teaching Program Schedule, October 2020

Time	Thursday	Friday	Saturday
10:00–11:00	ECD	ECD	
11:00–12:00	Literature in English 2 (SSS 1–3) Repeat	English Language 2 (SSS 1–3) Repeat	Chemistry (SSS 1–3)
12:00–13:00	Maths 1 (SSS 1–3) Repeat	English Language 1 (SSS 1–3) Repeat	Math 2 (SSS 1–3) Repeat
14:00–15:00	General Science (Pri) Grades 1–3	English (Pri) Grades 1–3	Math (Pri) Grades 1–3
15:00–16:00	General Science (Pri) Grades 4–6	English (Pri) Grades 4–6	
16:00–17:00	Integrated Science 2 (JSS 1–3)	Language Arts 2 (JSS 1–3)	
17:00–18:00	Social Studies/Civics (JSS 1–3)	French (JSS 1–3)	Home Economics (JSS 1–3)
18:00–19:00	Literature in English 2 (SSS 1–3)	English Language 2 (SSS 1–3)	Chemistry (SSS 1–3)
19:00–20:00	Maths (SSS 1–3)	English Language 2 (SSS 1–3)	Math (SSS 1–3)
20:00–20:30	Life Skills	Life Skills	
20:30–21:30	Maths (SSS 1–3) Repeat	English Language 2 (SSS 1–3) Repeat	

Source: MBSSE, Education Broadcasting House

The natural resources for generating electricity for about seven million people are abundant—solar, water, wind, and rubbish. The Bumbuna Hydroelectric Project is a water power plant that produces more than 50 percent of the energy supply in Sierra Leone. The project site is located near Bumbuna Falls on the upper reaches of the Seli/Rokel River, about 200 km Northeast of Freetown. Construction of the dam started in 1975 but, with 85 percent completion, work was halted in May 1997 as a result of the civil war. Work was completed in 2009 with assistance of the African Development Bank. It is estimated that the dilapidated national grid could only generate about 27 megawatts (electric output capabilities). A $6 million InfraCo Africa arrangement (Bumbuna Hydro II) was designed to modernize and increase output capacity to 143 megawatts.

There are indications that wind speeds of twelve meters per second are possible in parts of the country, implying that wind energy could be a viable option in selected locations. With the low-wind-speed turbines now available in the market, it has been projected that there is a strong potential for the use of wind-induced energy in the rural areas; especially in the north of the country. There is a known wind energy system of 5 kilowatts in Sierra Leone, located in the Bonthe District, along the south coastline area.[30]

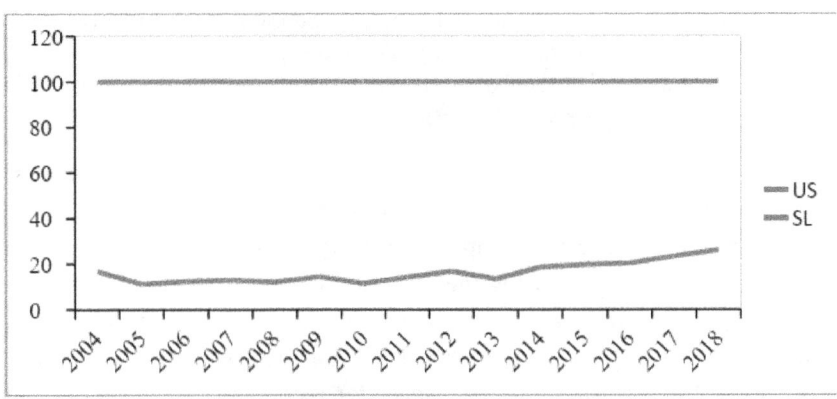

Figure 7.3: Access to Electricity
(Percent of the Population in the United States and Sierra Leone)
Data source: WDI (World Bank). Access to electricity is the percentage of the population with access to electricity. Electrification data are collected from industry, national surveys and international sources.

The energy revolution, which committed to reach 250,000 households with modern energy solutions by 2018, was belatedly launched in 2017. A collaborative public-private task force was established to focus on renewable energy, especially solar energy. By 2010, there was no solar power

30. See also https://energypedia.info/wiki/Sierra_Leone_Energy_Situation#Biomass.

capacity installed in Sierra Leone. Nevertheless, some bigger projects have been implemented from 2014 to 2018 (see Box 7.1): "According to the Ministry of Energy and Water Resources (MEWR), approximately 1460 kWh/mile of solar radiation can be expected annually in Sierra Leone."[31] What seems to be a more ambitious study by the Joint Research Centre (JRS) of the European Commission believes Sierra Leone's solar potential to be as high as 2200 kWh/m.[32] Rubbish, which is so prevalent in several areas of the country, can be converted into useful biomass energy (useful rubbish).

It is estimated that biomass energy accounts for 80 percent of energy consumption. The largest source of biomass energy is wood fuel, followed by charcoal,[33] which are both usually used hazardously and inefficiently. Scientists believe that there is considerable potential to produce biofuels from energy crops such as maize and cassava, and processing of charcoal into biochar without impacting food production. It is estimated that biomass could generate as much as 33 megawatts of energy.[34] The abysmal access to electricity can only be confounding, given the potential.

> The energy content of the total domestic and industrial refuse disposed of in 2012 amounted to 594,000 tons per annum. Options for energy production from municipal waste should be examined including biogas projects as well as methane gas from landfills.[35]

In the aftermath of the war and pandemics, structural problems continue to exist at the Collegiate School. Though the school has an electric grid, it does not have a generator to supply electricity or a solar panel facility. Toilet facilities were damaged during the war and need reinstallation. There were about twenty-six solid classrooms—albeit that two needed repairs—and 800 chairs in 2018. The library and science laboratories are somewhat functional. The school has a garden but not a space for recreation as it once did, and informal institutions are not permitted to use the facilities of the school.

31. See "Sierra Leone Energy Situation," para. 40.
32. See "Sierra Leone Energy Situation," para. 40.
33. See "Sierra Leone Energy Situation," para. 43; also see footnote 5.
34. See "Sierra Leone Energy Situation," para. 44.
35. See "Sierra Leone Energy Situation," para. 45. See also Renewable Energy Policy of Sierra Leone, 2016. It is reported that the Addax ethanol project, close to Makeni, uses sugar cane to produce bioethanol for export and domestic use and to supply the main Bumbuna-Freetown grid. Available power is estimated to be 15 megawatts. However, the company seemed to have suffered from some financial and operational troubles in 2015. The Magbass sugar cane industry in Port Loko district has also used bagasse to generate heat and electricity (see "Sierra Leone Energy Situation," paras. 46–47).

The Consequences of War and Pandemics (1991–2021)

At the time of this writing (2020), two principals are responsible for the administration of the school, Mr. Mohamed S. T. Koroma (SSS) and Mrs. Miranda Cole (JSS). As a result of the dissipation of the pressures of the war, the school does not operate dual-shifts at this time. The school retains its missionary status (with assistance). Data for 2018 indicate that the school had forty teachers and approximately 1,300 students (based on number of chairs). The pupil-teacher ratio can be estimated to be about 33:1, which is in excess of the national average.

National economic conditions and the lingering results of the civil war and Ebola have also affected the academic performance of the students. Students in the third year of senior secondary school are expected to take the West African Senior School Certificate Examination (WASSCE). Students take exams in nine subjects, which are split into two compulsory subjects (mathematics and English language) and seven subjects of the student's choice. Students can get a numeric grade ranging from 1 (Excellent) to 9 (Fail) for each subject.

The pass mark for each subject is 8. Students must pass at least five subjects (including mathematics or English language) with a numeric grade of 6 (Credit) or higher in order to qualify for university study. The overall pass mark for the WASSCE has been calculated here as being the difference between a score of 9 in nine subjects (eighty-one) and a score of 6 across five subjects (thirty), an overall score of 51 (Ministry of Basic and Secondary School Education [MBSSE]). The average scores of the Collegiate Students from 2016 to 2018 are reported in Figure 7.4.

The average scores are reminiscent of scores in the early 1970s (about 50 years ago) with a distinguishing feature of comparatively lower rates of success from 2016–18 (success rate of 2 to 3 percent of test takers). Invariably, the results are not very valuable without comparative analysis; that is, how are the other schools doing? There has been no evidence of transformational educational progress in a precarious educational environment with inadequate resources and infrastructure, and exogenous health and political disturbances.

The West African Methodist Collegiate School, 1911-2021

Box 7.1: Energy Projects (2014-18)

- Promoting Renewable Energy Services for Social Development (PRESSD) (2014-18): Installation and operation of three solar mini-grids in Segbwema, Panguma, and Gbinti, installation of SHS for approx. 100 charging centres, twenty energy hubs for Agricultural Business Centres, twenty clinics, twelve schools, twelve financial service associations. Equipment and training for three Energy Laboratories in cooperation with Polytechnics. Sales of Pico PV products through local retailers. Partners: European Union, Welthungerhilfe, Cooperazione Internationale, Energy for Opportunity, Oxfam.
- Rural Renewable Energy Project (2017-20): Installation of a total of fifty smaller (6-36 kilowatt) mini-grids and forty bigger (>36 kilowatt) mini-grids, located at health facilities. Development of private companies' operation model. Partners: UNOPS, UK Aid.
- Installation of Solar Street Lights: The Ministry of Energy Sierra Leone has installed 8471 solar street lights in the fourteen district headquarter towns across the country. The facilities were handed over to the various district councils, city councils, and local councils in 2017.
- The Ministry of Health is implementing the Expanded Program on Immunization and has installed approx. 900 solar-powered fridges, donated by UNICEF, since 2003 for the purpose of cooling vaccinations across the country. The program is currently replacing old fridges.

Smaller projects include:

- WASH Consortium: Implementation of solar water pumps for decentralized water supplies. Partners: DFID, Oxfam, Concern, Save the Children, Action against Hunger.
- Biodiversity Conservation Project: Solar charging centers to support Biodiversity Conservation. Partners: GEF, World Bank
- Apex Bank Solar Systems: Provision of SHS for Financial Service Associations and Community Banks. Partners: Kafeibu Constructions, IFAD.
- Advancing Partners and Communities: Solar systems for health facilities. Partners: USAID, JICA, JSI, ACF.
- Barefoot Women Solar College: Training center, courses for illiterate women, installation of solar systems for communities. Partners: Barefoot Women, Ministry of Energy.
- Playhouse Foundation/EnDev: SHS for health facilities and schools in Kono and Kailahun.
- Rural Energy Activating Livelihoods (REAL):Provision of electricity and employment options (charging center) to rural population. Partners. Environmental Foundation for Africa, EU.

Source: https://energypedia.info/wiki/Sierra_Leone_Energy_Situation#Biomass

* *The numbers of students who attempted the exam in chronological sequence were 210, 227, and 238. Data source: MBSSE*

The Consequences of War and Pandemics (1991-2021)

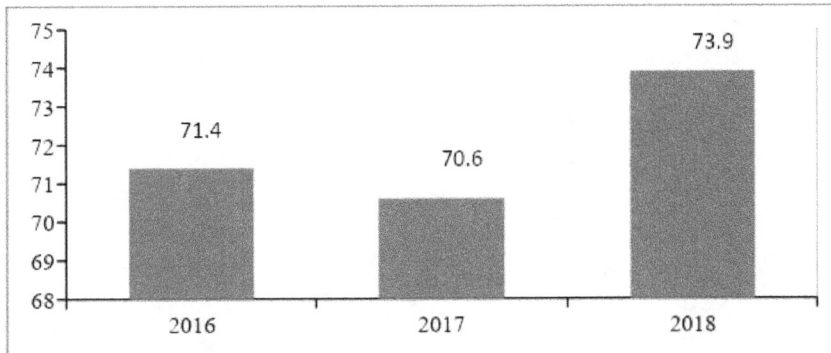

Figure 7.4: Average WASSCE grades (2016–18)*

Postscript

THE WAM COLLEGIATE SCHOOL is a product of missionary work. It had very precise Christian objectives when it was established in 1911, the education of students for the extension of missionary work as ministers, teachers, and civil servants. The school was established at a time when there was great interdenominational competition among the Christian Missionary Society (CMS), United Methodist Free Churches, the Wesleyan Methodists, and the West African Methodist (WAM) Church.

The establishment of schools in Freetown was a very revolutionary and expensive proposition, but the pioneers strongly believed in missionary work to improve the lives of Africans. As time went on, financing these institutions and churches became very exorbitant and the churches had to rely on governments and philanthropists to augment their expenditures. Yet the missionaries were passionate not only about providing parochial instruction but secular education that made education a pervasively functional undertaking. Old men made incredible and extraordinary sacrifices to ensure the continuity of their mission and objectives; so much so that the Collegiate School was rescued when it was on the verge of extinction.

The parochial schools made extraordinary contributions to the development of education in Sierra Leone, in particular, and West Africa, in general, by producing ministers, doctors, lawyers, teachers, medical professionals, and politicians who served the global community within and beyond the frontiers of Sierra Leone. The educators ventured into the nooks and crannies of territorial geography and braved the dangers of death in the interior of Sierra Leone and beyond.

Today, the mission of the Collegiate School is not radically or fundamentally different. The school provides both religious and secular education for the expansion of human capital against economic and social odds that

Postscript

are overpowering—political friction, poverty, income inequality, decrepit infrastructure, health challenges, and short life-expectancies. Contemporary education is no longer the proprietary right of any Christian denomination. Education is a merit good with positive externalities. Explicitly, it is the moral obligation of governments to educate their citizens.

When parochial institutions continue the noble endeavor of performing or augmenting a function of governments, governments must adequately reciprocate by supporting the institutions to the maximum extent possible; that is, governments must be invested and avid partners in the extension of education that is now a pale shadow of its former self. Evidently, the demand for missionary work and the spread of religion is no longer as rife as it was after 110 years.

Philanthropists, missionaries, and the Government of Sierra Leone must now be unrelenting partners in the spread of functional education that is so valuable to the reconstruction of Sierra Leone and Africa. Invariably, moral and social instruction has eternal values that cannot be perfected in any generation. Unavoidably, a concept that started over a hundred years ago is destined to outlast subsequent generations. We have only learnt that the challenges of preserving the concept are dynamic. While new infrastructural demands and fluidity show dynamic challenges confronting the essence of the school, the demand for financial commitments remain as sacrosanct as it was in 1911 and 1948; notwithstanding, the school continues to unwaveringly pursue its mission. The challenges need not be overpowering; for the school cannot go it alone! *Plus Ultra!*

Postscript

List of Principals of the WAM Collegiate School (1911–2021)

1911–15:	Rev. C. A. E Macauley; MBE, MA (Oxon)
1916–17:	Prof. O. Faduma; BD, PhD (Yale)
1917–23:	Rev. J. Brown-Nicols (Acting)
1923–27:	Rev. J. M. Aspansa Johnson; MA, DipTh (Dunelm), ACP
1948–65:	Mr. J. A. Garber; MA (Dunelm), LCP (London)
1966–71:	Mr. V. J. Hastings-Spaine; BA, DipEd (Dunelm), DipEd Admin (Reading)
1971–78:	Mr. L. B. Rogers Wright; BA (Dunelm), DipEd (USL), MEd (Bristol)
1975–77:	Mr. S. B. Moiba; BA, DipEd (Dunelm), ICE (Oxon; Acting)
1978–80:	Mr. B. A. King; BA, DipEd (Dunelm)
1980–98:	Rev. Z. S. Smith; BA, DipEd
1998–99:	Mr. S. E. Beury; BA, DipEd (Acting)
1999:	Mr. Nathaniel Davies; BA, DipEd
	Mrs. Veronica Perry, BEd, MEd
2019:	Aiah Kpakima
2020:	Mr. Mohamed S. T. Koroma (SSS)
	Mrs. Miranda Cole (JSS)

Appendix A

West African Methodist Collegiate School Song

1. The call has come to Afric's sons, to do and to endure.
   The light of knowledge and of power, she stands to spread abroad.
   Our hearts we raise in songs of praise, for wisdom's purest ray.
   While young and ole in joy acclaim, Collegiate Rah! Collegiate Rah!

2. A band of few have dared to raise, on this our sunny shore.
   The beam of Afric's dome sublime, supported by these four.
   Truth, justice, honour, love for all, in every age or clime.
   This home of learning shall upraise, the true Collegiate Rah! Rah! Rah!

3. No failure shall our course impede, no clouds our sky o'recast.
   Onward we move to victory, northwards we turn our steps.
   Till Afric's sons imbibe the best, of goodness and of peace.
   And fathers to their sons bequeath, the true Collegiate Rah! Rah! Rah!

4. Frankness and honour, reverence for all.
   Love for our fatherland, love for mankind.
   Joy in our country's good, wreaths for the great.
   This be thy character, O Collegiate Rah!
   These shall thy off-spring drink, from thy holy stream.
   O Rah Collegiate Rah! Rah! Rah!

Appendix A

5. Ye forward sons of yore, show us the way.

    Ye budding sons of Af', follow the path.

    The best that be in earth's domain, this Afric's sons shall prize.

    Till youths attain, to heights untrod, to realms unknown before.

    And see new vistas of renown, with the true,

    Collegiate Rah! Rah! Rah!

West African Methodist Collegiate School Song

Collegiate Rah!Rah!Rah!

Harmonised by Organists of the old boys association
UK branch; Christian Thomas, Ransford Grey, James Thorpe & Emerson Jackson.

Copyright ©WAMCS

Appendix A

West African Methodist Collegiate School Song

Appendix A

West African Methodist Collegiate School Song

Appendix B

[An unedited/original speech]

Speech delivered by Mr. J.A. Garber, MA (Dunelm), LCP. Principal of the WAM Collegiate School on the Occasion of the Official Opening of the New Collegiate School Buildings, Wilkinson Road, on Wednesday, 15th February, 1961.

YOUR EXCELLENCY....................

This is the first opportunity the West African Methodist Church is having to invite you within their own campus to an affair exclusively theirs. The Principal, Staff, and pupils of the Collegiate School, therefore, together with the Board of Governors feel proud that they have been accorded the distinguished honour of having you to take the leading part in the official opening of this School. In having you as head of affairs, we establish our loyalty to the Queen whom you represent, and under whose benign sovereignty this Colony has been happily governed. It is always a pleasure to this Colony to think that Her Majesty's Representative is keenly interested in our educational affairs, and, therefore, your acceptance of our invitation to take part in this official opening is regarded as a sure sign of that keen interest evinced in all educational institutions, whatever their size, and of the patronage which Sierra Leone has enjoyed from the United Kingdom.

The Rev. J. B. Nicols, a former Superintendent of this connexion was wont to remark that the schools are the nations' workshops. This statement seems to have a fresh meaning for us when we review your numerous activities in almost everyone of our Educational Institutions in your attempt to encourage, expand, maintain, and improve the various workshops in which are moulded the FUTURE citizens of Sierra Leone. In the past,

[An unedited/original speech]

other secondary schools have enjoyed your patronage. Today we can say the Collegiate School is not an exception. We take this opportunity also of welcoming Lady Dorman, well known for her interest in the Girl Guide Movement and British Red Cross Society, through whose unremitting care and attention, you have been equipped for your too numerous calls for service. It will be our pride to recall and even record that at the official opening of the Collegiate School, Sir Maurice Dorman, KCMG, Governor of Sierra Leone, and Lady Dorman, were present to grace the occasion and inspire those who engaged in one of the workshops of a people emerging into nationhood. We once more offer to you and Lady Dorman a cordial welcome.

The Principal, Staff, and pupils of the Collegiate School together with the Board of Governors extend a similar welcome to everyone in the gathering, fully assured that nothing short of interest in an African venture for the expansion and advancement of education had induced you to share with us the joy in an enterprise only just begun. It is a joy from a sense of achievement after years of struggle. This is a beginning of things, an endeavour, to preserve and improve on the past in keeping with the motto of our School, "PLUS ULTRA." Wishing always to move forward and march with the progress of the times, we can assure you that your confidence in the School will ever be maintained.

I must here introduce you to the place where we are all assembled. Fifty years ago when the first Collegiate School was opened, no one would have thought of building a school on this plot. It was the time when there was no Wilkinson Road and only a footpath lay between Congo Town and Lumley. This land was then wooded and was a favourite resort for hunters. In the Second World War the land was used as one of the military camps in Sierra Leone and was the scene of many military parades. After the military left it, its tall grass provided graze for cattle. Now the use of the land has improved. We feed our boys with food for mind and body. We drill them to become citizens and we hunt and sort the various types of intelligence for specific training.

This spot is well chosen—here is an extract from the Architect's report:

> The view of the land is superb as seen from site photographs, thee being an unobstructed view of Aberdeen Creek and Aberdeen Point with the open sea behind. There is a pleasant breeze going up and down all seasons of the year. The buildings stand having the hills in front and the sea behind them.

Appendix B

To justify our feeling of joy for this achievement, it might be well on this occasion for me briefly to relate the history of the school up to the present day. The WAM Church came into existence as a Lady Church in 1798 with powers to find churches and establish schools. In their desire to improve these institutions, the African members in 1821 appealed to the United Methodist Free Church in England for help. This help which was readily given covered training of Ministers in England, establishing Mission Stations in the Protectorate and running only elementary schools. In 1911, another appeal was made, the result of which was the founding of the UMC Collegiate School to train sons of the connexion particularly those who were to be ministers, teachers, and workers in the Colony and Protectorate Mission Stations.

The Rev. C. A. E. Macauley, who had just qualified as a graduate of Oxford, was appointed Principal of the School. With eight foundation pupils, this enthusiastic gentleman started to work on the first of June at No.8 Pademba Road, which continued to be the home of the School up to December 1927. Shortly after the founding of the School, a boarding house was started to meet the needs of pupils from the Gambia, Gold Coast [Ghana], Nigeria and the Protectorate of Sierra Leone. At the end of five years, the School was well established and drew its pupils from every corner of West Africa, and the Board of Governors at this stage acquired a land for a second building. Unfortunately, owing to some internal difficulties, the Rev. C. A. E. Macauley resigned his appointment and his post was filled by Professor Orishatukeh Faduma, a graduate of the University of Yale, The hard working gentleman with American background, did splendid work in the School for a short period of two years in which he served. After his resignation there followed an interregnum in which Rev. A. E. Greensmith and Rev. J. B. Nicols acted as Principals. In 1923, Rev. J. M. Asapansa Johnson, who had just returned to Freetown after completing his training in the University of Durham, was appointed Principal. The School continued for four years and closed down in December 1927. It is interesting to note that the first two Principals after their resignation from the service of the Collegiate School took up appointment as Inspector of Schools in the Education Department, the Rev. C. A. E. Macauley rose to the post of Assistant Director of Education. This gentleman is still alive and is Archdeacon of the Gambia and Rio Pongas.* In spite of the short existence of the School, it played an important part in the educational history of Sierra Leone by the evidence of the sound academic training and sportsmanlike

[*An unedited/original speech*]

character it offered to its pupils. To enable listeners to assess the work of the old Collegiate School, I would name a few of its alumni—Rev. W. E. A. Pratt, General Superintendent, Methodist Church; Rev. I. S. T. Fewry, General Superintendent, WAM Church; Dr. A. B. Abayomi-Cole, Principal Medical Officer, Sierra Leone; Tom Fowell Boston, Dental Surgeon in the United Kingdom, Barristers: Ronald and Singer Beoku-Betts; Mr. Hamble Johnson of Hamble-Noble Printing Works; Mr. Bunji-Thomas, ex-Deputy Harbour Master; Mr. V. E. J. Buckle of Audit Department; Mr. A. Alhadi, late Master of Court; Professor Williamson Taylor, MSc, Principal Mabang Agricultural College; Mr. Ralph James; Mr. R. D. Thomas, Sub-Manager Barclays Bank; Dr. Fashole-Luke, late Medical Officer; Mr. Lightfoot Taylor of Cable and Wireless; Mr. J. E. N. Campbell, Collector of Customs; Mr. J. B. Davies, MBE, formerly of the Medical Department; Mr. Eric Johnson of Castleton Elliott; Rev. T. J. V. Campbell, BA; Rev. E. A. E. Cole; Messrs. R. C. Barlatt and D. N. K. Browne; can I pass unmentioned the Hon. I. T. Wallace-Johnson, Member of the House of Representatives, and Councillor J. Galba-Bright, a prominent politician and businessman? Time and memory cannot allow me to mention others. The UMC Collegiate School came to a close after sixteen years of active life.

The closing of the School, however, did not erase it from the minds of the old boys and the Methodist Church. During the long sleep of the School for twenty-one years the Old Boys Committee was kept going and the WAM Church in its annual assembly reserved an item in its agenda for the Collegiate School, and these two bodies were largely responsible for the resuscitation of the School in 1948.

After going through the rigid formality of providing a suitable place for the school, a qualified Head and Staff, the Board of Governors were permitted by the Director of Education to re-open the Collegiate School on Tuesday 3rd February 1948; on that day forty pupils were enrolled in Prep. and Form one after taking a preliminary test. The next seven years of the School's history were years of struggle. The Collegiate School coming into existence after a long sleep of twenty-one years found it difficult to gain recognition from the older secondary schools. The Collegiate School was banned from School singing competition, Empire Day Sports, Common Entrance Examination, Cricket and Football [Soccer] League Competitions and Government Scholarships. This isolation made the Staff and pupils a sorry lot and the position was worsened by the absence of government subsidy to the School. For seven years the School was not put in the assisted list

Appendix B

and this in turn had its effect on the recruitment of Staff, and some members of the existing Staff withdrew their services. New ones were recruited only to withdraw after a term's service as the salary which the School could offer was small. The Board of Governors then invited a full dress inspection of the School by the Education Department. This was followed by another inspection of the School by the Minister of Education, Mr. A. M. Margai, whose prompt action on this occasion saved the life of the School, which was put down for a full grant in 1955. The School records its gratitude to this Hon. Member for giving it a new lease of life by providing for it a building grant, the result of which this occasion celebrates.

Recruitment of Staff

The new Collegiate School was faced with the problem of staffing. During this period of the School's history very few graduates came from Fourah Bay College and fewer still from overseas. From the start the School included in its course studies, science subjects. Science graduates were greatly in demand even in the United Kingdom. None could be recruited locally. Through the assistance of a devoted friend of the School, Miss Elizabeth Hurst, the Collegiate School was able to obtain a Science Master in the person of Mr. M. A. Hayes, who in spite of his handicap for equipment, laid the foundation for the study of Physics. The Board openly expresses its gratitude to this lady for her efforts in helping the course of education in this School.

With the receipt of government grant, the financial situation improved and one of the first steps of the Board was to acquire this land on which the School building now stands. This step made the School quite ready to use the building grant offered to it. The School is 300 strong and works up to School Certificate. The staffing position improved considerably at the beginning of the present academic year. This offers greater prospects for the future. Our physics, chemistry, and biology departments are manned by graduates.

Building

The sum of 72,000 pounds was used to put up the Science and classroom Blocks. Thanks to the UK Government for the Colonial Development and Welfare Fund and to the Sierra Leone Government for supplementing this

[An unedited/original speech]

grant. We are grateful to the architects and contractors for their work and the Education Department and the United Christian Council for their vigilance. These two buildings, however, fall short of what was proposed in the building plan. We need a place in which is centered the corporate life of the School; a workshop where we can sort out the future technicians whom Sierra Leone will need in the near future.

I cannot end without saying something about the Board of Governors. When I was appointed Principal of the School, I found out that the youngest of them was well over sixty years. The conditions under which they served were such as would frighten most people from offering their service as Board Members. They were expected to give counsel and sometimes to give money. This they did during the difficult days of the School when no government assistance was available. I must now close with a short anecdote depicting the service of the School Board. The re-opening of the School had already been fixed for 3rd February 1948, when instruction came from the Education Department to the General Superintendent to hold up arrangements until the Divisional Engineer pronounced the School suitable. The Board awaited the Engineer's decision with a heavy heart and on the day of inspection the Principal was alarmed to see a white man who gave a curt reply to his compliments and was unwilling to enter into conversation with him; a few minutes later after the arrival of the Engineer came the Director of Education, and then the Engineer, like an oracle, began to speak. These native posts must give way to iron columns, he said, looking at the posts which supported the School. These old men went to the Freetown Waterworks Department to get iron columns and within an hour they returned carrying these columns on their shoulders. One of them who is still alive is the person to unveil the second plaque. He is Brother J. T. Nottidge.

I have now given the preface to the history of an Institution, which by God's grace should outlive several generations of its sons. It is left for others to write the chapters one by one.

Once more in the name of the pupils and Staff with the Board of Governors of the Collegiate School, I welcome you all.

May I, at this point, make a special appeal to the Director of Medical and Sanitary Services. I am asking that a School Clinic be arranged somewhere near the Roosevelt School to serve the needs of the Collegiate School, Roosevelt, and Methodist Girls' High School. This will save the pupils the journey of over two miles to the School Clinic at Connaught Hospital. If this arrangement cannot be made at this moment, I would

Appendix B

suggest that visiting Dispensaries be sent round to the schools to deal with minor ailments. Vis, a Nursing Sister and a trained Nurse could travel in the morning from school to school and deal with such cases as are not serious. Serious cases could be sent to the hospital. This arrangement was working some time ago and proved very helpful to the schools in reducing the number of pupils who had to leave every morning for attendance at the Connaught Hospital.

*The Diocese of Gambia and The Rio Pongas was one of the five dioceses, along with Freetown, Niger, Accra, and Lagos, which formed the new Province of West Africa in 1981.

Appendix C

[An unedited/original speech]

SERMON PREACHED AT SAMARIA WAM Church, Waterloo Street, Freetown in onnection with the Diamond Jubilee of the W.A.M. Collegiate Schoolon Sunday May 30, 1971

    By the Rev. Dr. W. E. A. Pratt OBD, MA
    (Ex-President of the Methodist Conference)
    Text: Acts 9.6 .... "Lord, what wilt thou have me to do?"
    Acts 2.37 .... "What shall we do?"

I congratulate you Principal, Staff (Present and Past) Pupils (Present and Past) Members of the Board of Governors of the West African Methodist Collegiate School and I join with you in thanking God who has brought the School to its sixtieth year, its Diamond Jubilee.

This is the third or fourth time I have been spared and privileged to preach the Thanksgiving Sermon of my alma mater—the Collegiate School.

I want to ask a simple question this afternoon which I am almost sure you will be able to answer, and that question is, how old are you?

    Twelve years? No .... thirteen? ....
.... fourteen?
.... fifteen? ....
.... nineteen years?

You are more than twelve, (thirteen, fourteen .... nineteen).

You are sixty years old, all of you, and the reason is that the experience which the school has passed through and acquired is yours by heritage.

Appendix C

We are proud of the Collegiate School or at least we ought to be, because it is the only school I know that was dead and is alive, the only school that has experienced a resurrection. It was born in 1911, died in 1927 and rose again in 1948. Since you cannot divorce its former life and experience from its latter, the school is now sixty years old and that is how and why you are celebrating the Diamond Jubilee of the school i.e. why you are sixty years old.

I have told you that the Collegiate School was born in 1911, i.e., it came into being in 1911. It died in 1927 i.e. it closed in 1927 when it was sixteen years old. It rose again in 1948 after twenty-one years of strain and struggle to have it resurrected.

During the first part of its history, it had as Principals distinguished pedagogues like the Rev. C. A. E. Macauley, MA, who subsequently became 1st African Assistant Director of Education and later still Archdeacon of Guinea, Gambia, [and] Rio Pongas Guinea. Then later doctor Orishatukeh Faduma, PhD of Yale University, USA. He subsequently entered government service. The finally Rev. J. M. Asapansa Johnson, MA, ACP. The school closed down because of mismanagement and some unfortunate circumstances.

During this period of hibernation, the Old Boys or some Old boys and some Members of the Board of Governors did not go into winter quarters; they did not give sleep to their eyes nor slumber to their eyelids, but kept on thinking and planning until God sent a man, J. A. Garber Esq. MA, LCP, who joined forces with the Revs. J. Brown-Nicols, EAE Cole, brethren J. T. Nottidge, J. G. Hyde, BL; R. I. A. Aubee; D. A. Williams; J. Adjai Thomas, and others latterly, and so the school was born again and it had its second birthday in 1948. All praise and thanks to God and the brethren aforementioned. It was an uphill task, it was a big and long struggle for government recognition and even recognition of the other secondary schools.

The Principal, J. A. Garber, Esq. in his address delivered on the official opening of the school on Wednesday 15th February 1961, said inter alia:

> The next seven years of the School's history were years of struggle. The Collegiate School coming into existence after a long sleep of 21 years found it difficult to gain recognition from the older secondary schools. The Collegiate School was banned from School singing competition, Empire Day Sports, Common Entrance Examination, Cricket and Football [Soccer] League Competitions and Government Scholarships. This isolation made the Staff and pupils a sorry lot and the position was worsened by the absence of Government subsidy to the School. For seven years the School

[An unedited/original speech]

was not put in the assisted list and this in turn had its effect on the recruitment of Staff, and some members of the existing Staff withdrew their services.

After facing and solving all the teething problems and with government grant coming in the Board of Governors was able to acquire land on which the new school now stands at Wilkinson Road on the Western side of Freetown. Building grants came in bit and the present school buildings were put up with physics, chemistry, and biology departments. Mr. Garber labored for seventeen years as Principal of the Collegiate School and handed over to another worthy and distinguished son of the soil, Mr. V. J. Hastings-Spaine, BA, DipEd in 1966. He held the fort for five years now meeting and tackling not the teething problems, but the common complicated problems of indiscipline, violence, unruliness, etc. A little bird is whispering but I can't hear what the whisper is. I hope however it is not true. Be that as it may, I wish the Principal all success and God's blessing and guidance, I appeal to the Old Boys especially to rally round the Principal and their Alma Mater and give her greater patronage, recognition and service (I am not satisfied at the number of Old Boys that turns out on Thanksgiving and other occasions . . . .).

The pith of this sermon is to lead you to ask the one question in our text. There are two questions, but the two are one. The first is (Acts 9:6) Lord, what wilt Thou have me to do? In other words Saul was asking Jesus Christ: What shall I do? The Second (Acts 2:37) is a straight personal question in plural, the congregation were asking Peter and John, What shall we do? But before I put the question to you I would like to draw your attention to some facts and figures:

When I was a pupil at the Collegiate School in 1915, I cannot tell you how many primary or elementary schools were in Sierra Leone. But from figures obtained from the Ministry of Education:

Now there are 102 . . . . in the Western Area

Now there are 385 . . . . in Southern Province

Now there are 273 . . . . in Eastern Province

Now there are 263 . . . . in Northern Province

Making a total of 1023.

Appendix C

Secondary Schools: There were about nine in the whole of Sierra Leone about 1915. The number of pupils was not more than 150 to 200 at most in each school. Now listen; there are ninety-one in the whole country:—

Western Area	25
Southern Province	31
Northern Province	16
Eastern Province	19
Training Colleges	
Western Area	2
Southern Province	2
Eastern Province	1
Northern Province	3
Technical Institutes	2
Trade Centres	2

I want you to do a bit of thinking and imagination. Some of these ninety-one secondary schools have over 600 pupils, others of course have less. Suppose we give each 300 pupils, then we must assume that over (19 x 20) 380 pupils are leaving school each year; if say 400 boys and girls are leaving school each year, here comes our question, what are they to do? They must be serious minded enough to ask themselves individually and collectively, what shall I do? What shall we do?

Employment is the burning question.

I have come to the conclusion that some people are unemployable; they cannot be employed; in other words they don't want to work . . . . (I)

House boy . . . . (II) men going around with a dozen or two kola-nuts for sale. . . .I had purposed to stress the subject of Agriculture in this sermon, but I heard a talk over the radio which told me of a sad disappointment of youths who were trained and qualified at Njala College [an agricultural college], and yet have no work to do, no employment. If this is correct, it has to be quickly looked into. Cabinet Ministers after Cabinet Ministers have stressed the importance of agriculture in Sierra Leone.

Agriculture is important not only to Sierra Leone, but the whole world. It is said that an army marches on its stomach:

we say empty gun nor bar fire [a gun without ammunition is useless], empty bag cannot stand up. Farming, agriculture is the first

[An unedited/original speech]

work that God gave to man; for Adam and Eve were put in the Garden of Eden, they were put there to dress and to keep it. It is not a good sign for the country when everybody who can read A, B, C, or write a letter wants to join the white collared job . . . . to become a clerk.

Farming or agriculture supplies food to the farmer and employment to himself. My late father was a farmer not in the mechanized or scientific sense, but in the ordinary sense, and yet he was able to bring up his family of seven boys on his farming. When I visited England, the late Rev. J.J. Whitfield took me around and I met two farmers who were almost millionaires each and they were highly respected above and beyond many white collared jobbers and lawyers and doctors. Even if what is said about students qualified in Njala is true, some of us ought to begin to make the sacrifice in agriculture and farming; without shedding of blood there is no remission of sin, without sacrifice and self-denial we cannot get on in this world of ours; and here the philosophy of One Country, One People comes in handy since the land in the province is more fertile than the land in the Western Area . . . . We can do a lot from small beginning and sacrifice and self-denial "Little drops of water, little grains of sand, make the mighty ocean and the beauteous land.

We may not appreciate this because of the insatiable desire to get rich quick, overnight, without much toil and work, but it is one way out of the unemployment consequent upon the number of boys and girls leaving school every year at the moment.

This get rich quick does not help us in our trade also. We do not believe in a quick cent rather than in a slow five cents . . . . This lack of sacrifice and self-denial; this get rich quick business also militates against our answering God's call and offering for the Ministry of the Church.

I have not come to you with any high sounding or elaborate philosophy. Many times such a philosophy fails to hit the mark and to accomplish that which is desired . . . . That, I take it, is the meaning of the story of the student and the ferryman . . . . do you know Psychology? No, then one-fourth of your life is gone. Philosophy? No; Theology? No; then another one-fourth of your life is gone. Then a threatened storm. The ferryman was frightened and asked the student: do you know Swimology? No, answered the student; then the whole of your life is gone.

Appendix C

We may be ever so clever and learned, we may know all the *Ologies* and all the Latin and Greek, etc., and fail in the common practical things of life on which our existence and life depends.

Some long, long, years ago I read a story of a man, Dick Whintonting, who was leaving London, downcast and brokenhearted and in despair, a voice said to him, "turn again Dick Whintonting, Lord Mayor of London," God's voice is coming to us in various ways; "Come unto me, all ye that labour and are heavy laden and I will give you rest.".......... That is God's call to man, God's Call to the world. We have problems, we have difficulties; of ourselves we cannot solve them, we cannot overcome them, but God can and He invites you to come unto Him and He will help you, He will guide you and direct you and show you what you will do and what you can do, and where you will go..............................

Bibliography

Alghali, Aliyageen M., et al. "Education in Sierra Leone with Particular Reference to Open and Distance Learning and Information and Communication Technologies." Presentation given at the national forum for the Commonwealth of Learning, Freetown, Sierra Leone, February 16–18, 2005. http://oasis.col.org/bitstream/handle/11599/187/SierraLeone_EnviroScan.pdf;sequence=.

Alison-Konteh, I. "The Changing Phase of the WAM Collegiate School." *The Sierra Leonean*, January 21, 1965.

———. "Sir Albert Presides over Speech Day Ceremony." *The Sierra Leonean*, January 21, 1965.

Campbell, Greg. *Blood Diamonds*. Cambridge, MA: Basic, 2004.

Cennimo, David J. "What Is COVID-19?" https://www.medscape.com/answers/2500114-197401/what-is-covid-19.

Coupland, Reginald. *The British Antislavery Movement*. London: Butterworth, 1933.

Deveneaux, Gustav H. K. "Faduma, Orishatukeh." In *Dictionary of North Carolina Biography*, edited by William S. Powell, n.p. 6 vols. Chapel Hill: University of North Carolina, 1979–96. https://www.ncpedia.org/biography/faduma-orishatukeh.

Dougherty, Beth K. "Searching for Answers: Sierra Leone's Truth and Reconciliation Commission." *African Studies Quarterly* 8.1 (2004) 39–56.

Fofana, Umaru. "Sierra Leone Schools Reopen after Long Closure Due to Ebola." *Reuters*, April 14, 2015. https://www.reuters.com/article/us-health-ebola-leone-education/sierra-leone-schools-reopen-after-long-closure-due-to-ebola-idUSKBN0N51JY20150414.

Foray, Cyril P. *Historical Dictionary of Sierra Leone*. Metuchen, NJ: The Scarecrow, 1977.

Fyfe, Christopher. *Sierra Leone Inheritance*. London: Oxford University, 1964.

Fyle, Magbaily C. *Historical Dictionary of Sierra Leone*. Lanham, MD: The Scarecrow, 2006.

Hoffman, Danny. "The Civilian Target in Sierra Leone and Liberia: Political Power, Military Strategy, and Humanitarian Intervention." *African Affairs* 103 (2004) 211–26.

Jackson, Emerson A. "Proposal for Virtual ICT Use in Sierra Leone Education System: A Case of MOODLE." *Journal of Applied Thought* 1.5 (2016) 79–94.

Keen, David. *Conflict and Collusion in Sierra Leone*. London: Currey, 2005.

King, Emmanuel L. R. "A History of the Sierra Leone Grammar School 1845–Present." BA Hons. diss., Fourah Bay College, University of Sierra Leone, Freetown, 1984.

Labor, Clarence E. A. No title. *Daily Mail*, January 28, 1970.

Mathieson, Willian L. *British Slavery and Its Abolition, 1823–1838*. London: Octagon, 1926.

Bibliography

———. *Great Britain and the Slave Trade*. London: Longmans & Green, 1929.

Matsumoto, Mitsuko. "Young People, Education, and the 'New' Wars: The Case of Sierra Leone." *Infancia Contemporánea* 6 (2014) 100–117.

Mellor, George R. *British Imperial Trusteeship, 1783–1850*. London: Faber & Faber, 1951.

Metzger, Sam. No title. *Unity*, January 28, 1970.

Moiba, Solomon. "A History of the Collegiate School, Freetown 1911–1965." BA dip. ed., diss., Fourah Bay College-Durham, Freetown-London, 1966.

Momodu, Samuel. "The Sierra Leone Civil War (1991–2002)." *Black Past*, January 16, 2017. https://www.blackpast.org/global-african-history/sierra-leone-civil-war-1991-2002/.

Moore, Moses N. *Orishatukeh Faduma, Liberal Theology and Evangelical Pan-Africanism 1857–1946*. London: Scarecrow, 1996.

Okonkwo, Rina L. "Orishatukeh Faduma: A Man of Two Worlds." *The Journal of Negro History* 67.1 (1983) 24–36.

Omer-Cooper, John D., et al. *The Growth of African Civilization: The Making of Modern Africa to the Partition*. Singapore: New Art Printing, 1972.

Ozisik, Shenel. "Education in Sierra Leone." *The Borgen Project*, January 25, 2015. https://borgenproject.org/education-sierra-leone/.

Penrose, B. *Travel and Discovery in the Renaissance 1420–1620*. Cambridge, MA: Harvard University, 1963.

Porter, Arthur. *Creoledom*. London: Oxford University, 1963.

Pratt, Akinumi W. E. *Autobiography*. Freetown: Government Printing, 1973.

Pugel, Thomas A. *International Economics*. 16th ed. New York: McGraw Hill, 2016.

Rodney, Walter. *How Europe Underdeveloped Africa*. Washington, DC: Howard University, 1982.

Sachs, Jeffrey D. "How to Handle the Macroeconomics of Oil Wealth." In *Escaping the Resource Curse*, edited by Marcatan Humphreys et al., 173–93. New York: Columbia University, 2007.

———. "What Is the Role of the State?" In *Escaping the Resource Curse*, edited by Marcatan Humphreys et al., 23–52. New York: Columbia University, 2007.

Shakespeare, William. *The Complete Works: Compact Edition*. Edited by Gary Taylor et al. Oxford: Claredon, 1988.

Shodekeh-Johnson, F. "The Growth and Development of the West African Methodist Church." PhD diss., Freetown, University of Sierra Leone, 1980.

"Sierra Leone." http://uis.unesco.org/en/country/sl.

"Sierra Leone Energy Situation." https://energypedia.info/wiki/Sierra_Leone_Energy_Situation.

Sifferlin, Alexandra. "5 Million Kids Aren't in School Because of Ebola." *TIME*, December 17, 2014. https://time.com/3637570/5-million-kids-arent-in-school-because-of-ebola/.

Simeon, James. L. "Faduma Orishatukeh (A)." *Dictionary of African Christian Biography*, n.p. 2002. https://dacb.org/stories/sierra-leone/faduma-orishatukeh/.

Stiglitz, Joseph. "What Is the Role of the State?" In *Escaping the Resource Curse*, edited by Marcatan Humphreys et al., 23–52. Initiative for Policy Dialogue at Columbia. New York: Columbia University, 2007.

Stiglitz, Joseph, and Shari Spiegel. "Series Preface." In *Escaping the Resource Curse*, edited by Marcatan Humphreys et al., v–vi. New York: Columbia University, 2007.

Bibliography

Sumner, Doyle L. *Education in Sierra Leone*. Freetown: The Government of Sierra Leone, 1963.
West African Methodist Collegiate School. *The Collegiate Diamond Jubilee Handbook 1911–1971*. Freetown, 1971.
Williams, Eric. *Capitalism and Slavery*. Chapel Hill, NC: The University of North Carolina, 1994.
Warburton, Christopher E. S. *The Evolution of Crises and Underdevelopment in Africa*. Lanham, MD: University Press of America, 2005.
"World Development Indicators." https://datacatalog.worldbank.org/dataset/world-development-indicators.
"Youth/Adult Literacy Rate." http://uis.unesco.org/en/glossary-term/youthadult-literacy-rate.

Index

Aberdeen Village, 29, 47, 103, 139
Albert Academy, 8, 15, 30, 47, 84
American Methodist Episcopal, 8
Annie Walsh Memorial School, 8
Assembly Hall, 49, 53–54, 56, 68, 77, 92

Basic Education Certificate Examination (BECE), 105
Beckley, A.O., 55, 59
biomass, 122, 123, 125,
Black Poor, 3–4
Boarding Department, 28–30
Bright-Leigh, T.J., 17–18
Brookfields, 25
Browne, James, Rev., 12
Brown-Nicols, J.B. Rev., 20, 27, 56, 70, 129, 146
Bumbuna Falls, 122–22
Butcher, Janet, Mrs., 32

Campbell, T.J.V., 29
Christian Missionary Society (CMS), 8, 10, 127,
CMS Grammar School, 13, 17, 19–21, 28, 30, 35, 58, 71, 88,
Circular Road, 32, 35, 36–57, 69–70, 87–88, 91
Civil War, 6, 91, 103–5, 106–14, 121, 123
Clarkson, T.W., 18–19, 25–26, 29, 69
Cole, E.A.E., 17–18, 30, 54, 66, 69, 141, 146
Colonial Development and Welfare Fund, 48, 142
Congo Town, 7, 47, 139

COVID-19, 106, 113, 115–16, 118

Dallimore, Henry, Rev., 21
Davies, C.A., 32, 39, 43
Davies, J.A.D., Rev., 18, 19, 54, 99, 103
Diamond Jubilee, 13–14, 16, 18, 20, 26, 35–36, 38, 59, 65–70, 145–46
Dorman, Maurice, Sir. (Governor), 50–51, 139
Dress Reform Society, 15

Ebola, 106, 113–16, 118, 123
Eckett, Robert, Rev., 12
Empire Day, 25, 141, 146

Faduma, Orishatukeh, Rev., 14–16, 21–26, 68, 96, 100, 129, 140, 146
Fewry, I.S.T., Rev., 17–18, 30, 50, 52–53, 68, 70, 90, 141
Foundation Day, 66, 68, 100
Foundation students, 17–18, 34, 36, 68, 140
Fourah Bay College, 16, 18, 25, 27, 32, 35, 43, 55, 58, 64, 69, 72, 78, 84, 88, 91
Foya, Sahr, 39
Frankpledge, 3

Galba-Bright, J., 68, 70, 141
Garber, J.A., (Principal), 30, 35–59, 129, 138–47
General Certificate Examinations (GCE), 45, 59, 61, 64, 65, 73, 83–84, 90, 96, 102–3, 105

Index

GloucesterVillage, 29
Government Assisted Schools, 32, 36, 40–41, 43

Hamilton Village, 26–27, 29
Hanway, Jonas, 3
Hastings-Spaine, V. Rev. (Principal), 43, 55–56, 58–72, 87, 100, 129, 147
Hill Station, 26, 29
Hogbrook; see Wilberforce
Hundredor, 3

Interregnum, 30, see also Garber

Johnson, Asapansa, Rev. (Principal), 16, 140, 146,

King, B.A. (Principal), 32, 43–44, 55, 58, 84, 87–90

Liberated Africans; see Recaptives
Literary and Debating Society(L&DS), 36, 45, 73, 76–77, 100
Luke, S.E., 48–49

MaCarthy, Charles, (Governor), 7–8, 10
Macauley, C.E.A., (Principal), 13, 16, 17–20, 24, 56, 68, 129, 140, 146
Mansfield, Chief Justice, 2,
marching band, 59, 66–67, 80, 83, 98–100
Margai, A.M. (Hon.), 44, 48, 50, 55, 142
Maroons, 6
Micklethwaite, W. Rev., 27
Moiba, S.B., 28–29, 32, 41–45, 59–62, 64, 78–80, 82–83, 85–88, 93, 97, 99, 103, 129
Momoh, J.S. (President), 45, 87, 98–99, 103–4, 106, 108

National Provisional Ruling Council (NPRC), 104, 108
New, Joseph, Rev., 12
Nova Scotians, 5–6, 11
Number Two Village, 26–27

O'Connor, Anthony, 11

Pademba Road, 13, 19, 24, 68, 140
Palmer, Andrew, 17–18
pandemics see also COVID-19 and Ebola
Parent-Teacher Association (PTA), 78–80, 92–94, 99, 100
Penny Day, 19
Plus Ultra, see School's crest
Pratt, Moses, 17
Pratt, W.E.A., Rev., 17–18, 25, 27, 29, 54, 67, 141, 145–50
Public Works Department (PWD), 48–49, 53

Quit rents, 6

Recaptives, 5–8, 10–11
Revolutionary United Front (RUF), 106–9
Rice, Mr., 33
Rogers-Wright, L. (Principal), 71–89, 100, 129
Rogers-Wright, Cyril, 47
Rollings, C.M.A., 17–18

Samaria Church, 13, 65–68, 145
School's crest, 37–39
School's song, 39, 81, 131, 133–37
scouting, 25–26, 77–78, 100
Sharp, Granville, 2–4, 6
Sierra Leone Company, 5–6
St. George's Bay Company, 4–5
Smeathman, H., 3
Smith, Rev.Z.S.F., 85–87, 90–106, 129
solar energy, 121–24
Soldier Street, 13, 24, 28
Somerset, James, 2,
Sussex Village, 26–27, 29

Teaching Service Commission, 119–20
Tithingman/men , 3
Thorpe, J.R.T., 27, 79–80, 93, 99, see also PTA
Tokeh Village, 26–27, 29
Tower Hill, 25, 29
Trotter, Rev., 12

Index

United Methodist Free Churches, 10–12, 14, 20

Wallace-Johnson, I.T.A.. 13, 18, 59, 70, 99, 141
Warboys, C. Rev., 12
Warburton, C.E.S., 97, 107
Waterloo Village, 14, 17–18, 34–35
West African Methodists, 20, 33–34
Wesleyan Methodists, 11, 28, 127

West African Secondary School Certificate Examination (WASSCE), 105, 123, 125
Wilberforce, 7, 17–19
Wilkinson Road, 35, 45–57, 91, 95, 113–14, 138–39, 147

York Village, 17–18, 26–27, 29

Zuzay, Mr., 47

www.ingramcontent.com/pod-product-compliance
Lightning Source LLC
Chambersburg PA
CBHW051936160426
43198CB00013B/2178